Working with
Youth-at-Risk
in Hong Kong

Hong Kong University Press thanks Xu Bing for writing the Press's name in his Square Word Calligraphy for the covers of its books. For further information, see p. iv.

To Professor Keith Bottomley,
my mentor and friend

Working with
Youth-at-Risk
in Hong Kong

Edited by Francis Wing-lin Lee

香港大學出版社

HONG KONG UNIVERSITY PRESS

Hong Kong University Press
14/F Hing Wai Centre
7 Tin Wan Praya Road
Aberdeen
Hong Kong

ISBN 962 209 761 8

Cover photographs courtesy of
The Hong Kong Federation of Youth Groups

Secure On-line Ordering
http://www.hkupress.org

British Library Cataloguing-in-Publication Data
A catalogue record for this book is available
from the British Library.

Printed and bound by HeterMedia Services Ltd., in Hong Kong, China

Hong Kong University Press is honoured that Xu Bing, whose art
explores the complex themes of language across cultures, has written
the Press's name in his Square Word Calligraphy. This signals our
commitment to cross-cultural thinking and the distinctive nature
of our English-language books published in China.

"At first glance, Square Word Calligraphy appears to be nothing more
unusual than Chinese characters, but in fact it is a new way of
rendering English words in the format of a square so they resemble
Chinese characters. Chinese viewers expect to be able to read Square
Word Calligraphy but cannot. Western viewers, however are
surprised to find they can read it. Delight erupts when meaning is
unexpectedly revealed."

— Britta Erickson, *The Art of Xu Bing*

Contents

Foreword

It was more than thirty years ago that I started my career as a social worker. My first job was with the Government's Social Welfare Department and my assignment was to work as a Probation Officer to serve the Juvenile Court. At that time, we were already using the term "youth-at-risk", though its Chinese equivalent, "feizai", referred to youths whose social behaviours were not so acceptable. Since then, I have always been puzzled over what the term "youth-at-risk" actually means, as I believe young people are often a bit wayward in their behaviour and are at risk of offending the law.

In 1977, a Green Paper on "Personal Social Work among Young People" was published, and formally used the term "youth-at-risk" to refer to some young people who were thought to have the need for social work services. In order to meet their needs, a whole range of social work services, including school social work, outreaching social work, and family life education, was initially recommended. These have since become the mainstay of our youth services. However, questions over the definition of "youth-at-risk" have been raised since it was first used in the Green Paper. For example, critics were quick to point out that the Green Paper's estimation that only about one percent of the secondary school students were deemed "youth-at-risk" is actually a gross estimation, and that this reflected no more than the limited social work resources provided by the government.

In the mid-1980s, I was invited by the Tsuen Wan District Board to conduct research to look at the problem of delinquent youth. At that time, Hong Kong people were more receptive of the anti-social behaviour of young people, and was less ready to classify them as "youth at-risk".

In fact, the term "youth-at-risk" had begun to take on a narrower definition and was only applied to those who had done something contrary to the law, although this did not necessarily translate into judicial actions being taken against them. This restricted way of understanding the term made its meaning clearer, but it excluded, at the same time, a large number of young people who would have the same need for social work services but were not delinquent enough to fall into the "youth-at-risk" category.

During the 1990s, while serving as a Youth Commission member, my attention was shifted to the so-called "normal" youth, who, by definition, had not violated the law. The question I often asked myself during that period was: are these young people truly not at-risk? The dividing line was certainly not so clear cut. I understand that some young people were classified as "youth-at-risk", only because the Government had wanted to concentrate its limited social work resources on those whose needs appeared most apparent.

But is there a better way of deploying our social work resources which would not necessarily require the division of our young people into two different groups? The integrated model, proposed in the mid-1990s, combining the various social work services for young people, answered my query and represented an attempt to remove the boundary that had been arbitrary from the start. With implementation of the integrated model in recent years, all young people can now make use of a service that is essential to their development.

With the removal of the boundary, is there still a need to classify some young people as "youth-at-risk"? I think we probably have to. Although social work services are now available to all young people, since their needs are different, special services have to be designed for different groups, such as the "youth-at-risk". Given the fact that social work resources are always short in supply, the setting of priorities, whereby we target our services on those with the greatest need, will always be a timely strategy. In other words, we still need to identify the young people most at risk and offer them assistance. The task has, however, become even more difficult, as we now have to justify why some young people deserve more of our attention than others.

The chapters in this book, edited by Dr. Francis Wing-lin Lee, is an attempt to address this daunting task. I am happy that the range of contributors includes not only academics, who often tend to have a theoretical approach, but also practitioners, who work day and night with young people. While the authors may not have a better way of defining "youth-at-risk", I am sure, from their research and practical experiences, they will go far enough in pointing the way to make better use of our social work resources for young people.

Professor Nelson Wing-sun Chow
Department of Social Work and Social Administration
The University of Hong Kong

Preface

A colloquial term for "Youth-at-risk" is "Marginal youth". It connotes "standing on the edge of becoming a juvenile delinquent". This type of young people are considered quite risky as they are likely to break the law and could become official delinquents. Around 6,000 juveniles (7-15) have been arrested each year over the past 10 years (Commissioner of Police, 1993-2002), according to statistics from the Hong Kong Police. Although not all arrested young people have been convicted as official delinquents, the figures, to a certain extent, reveal a large portion of society's young population are marginalized.

The youth-at-risk problem has drawn much attention and concern from the public and the government. Various Western and local theories have been put forward to account for the youth-at-risk or juvenile delinquent problem (Cohen, 1955; Dryfoos, 1990; Glueck and Glueck, 1956; Lee, 2002; McWhirter, 1998; Morris, 1957; Schoenfeld, 1975 & Sutherland, 1939). But various concerned parties are still focused on tackling the issue of reducing the problem. Some commonly recognize categories of at-risk youth as youth gangs, young substance abusers, school bullies and cautioned juveniles. These young people are usually perceived as impulsive-natured individuals rather than hard core criminals, and need the help of welfare services rather than punishment.

The organization of this book is as follows. After introducing the local phenomena of youth-at-risk in Chapter 1, different services for these young people will be presented in Chapter 2. A central aim of this book is to introduce different intervention approaches, for working with different categories of at-risk young people. These approaches will be discussed in Chapters 3 to 7. The effectiveness of youth-at-risk services will be discussed in Chapter 8 through examples such as Outreaching Social Work Service – street work with unattached youth.

Chapter 9 is an enlightening chapter making the argument that the youth problem is a socially constructed phenomenon from our risky society. Based on this proposition, some reflections of our work with youth-at-risk are made. At the end of the day, the youth-at-risk problem does exist, regardless of what propositions we believe in. So, in the concluding chapter (Chapter 10), principles and the future direction of working with youth-at-risk are shared.

Aside from sharing different working approaches, it is hoped this book can stimulate our thoughts in innovating and designing effective working approaches with this group of young people, in order to help them better integrate into our society and lead a healthy life.

As a concluding remark, it has to be mentioned that the theories employed in different chapters of this book are developed in the Western world. But it is believed that these concepts can be applied in Hong Kong, a non-Western setting. To apply these ideas in a non-Western setting helps to reinforce a cross-cultural understanding of the issues discussed.

Contributors

Francis Wing-lin Lee   Associate Professor
Department of Social Work and Social
Administration
The University of Hong Kong

Cecilia Wing-yin Ho   Former Unit-in-charge
Beat Drugs Counselling and Education
Project (VCD Project)
The Hong Kong Federation of Youth Groups

Dennis Sing-wing Wong   Associate Professor
Department of Applied Social Studies
The City University of Hong Kong

Sindy Sin-ting Lee   Centre-in-charge
Centre for Restoration of Human
Relationships

Karen A. Joe Laidler   Associate Professor
Department of Sociology
The University of Hong Kong

Koon-mei Lee   Team Leader
Project Phoenix
Methodist Centre

Howard Chi-ho Cheng   Associate Professor
Department of Applied Social Sciences
The Hong Kong Polytechnic University

Sammy Wai-sang Chiu   Associate Professor
Department of Social Work
The Hong Kong Baptist University

1

Introduction:
The Phenomena of "Youth-at-Risk" in Hong Kong

Francis Wing-lin Lee

From a developmental perspective, every one of us has different developmental tasks to fulfill at different stages in the life process and is prone to be at risk if the tasks are not fulfilled/satisfied. But why are young people or adolescents usually regarded as more at risk? Young people are typically perceived as immature, with low self-esteem, lack of coping ability and self-control (Dryfoos, 1990; Jessor et al., 1991; McWhirter et al., 1998). When youth-at-risk (YAR) is mentioned, it is usually associated with young people in the education system who are on the fringe of dropping out of schools (Capuzzi & Gross, 1996). McWhirter et al. (1998) provided a comprehensive definition of "at-risk". They defined "at-risk" as:

> A set of presumed cause-and-effect dynamics that place the child or adolescent in danger of negative future events ... a situation that is not necessarily current but that can be anticipated in the absence of intervention (P.7).

Under this definition, we can understand that, for example, young people who exhibit aggression (cause) run the risk of exhibiting anti-social behaviour (effect) if no appropriate intervention is provided. Young people who exhibit anti-social behaviour (cause) run the risk of committing delinquency (effect) if no appropriate intervention is provided. They further propose a five-tier at-risk continuum for young people. It ranges from minimal risk to remote risk, high risk, imminent risk to the ultimate at-risk category (McWhirter et al., 1998:7–9). Young people belonging to different at-risk levels have different socio-economic profiles. Lee (1994) mentioned some characteristics specific to different YAR groups. These include existing in natural groupings, strong group cohesion, distinct subculture and exhibiting pro-delinquent/delinquent behaviour.

People often associate at-risk youth in Hong Kong with youth gangs/ street youth, young substance abusers, school dropouts and young delinquents. As an introduction to this book, this chapter will present some phenomena of these groupings so that readers can acquire some basic understanding of their situations in the local context.

Youth Gangs

Whenever youth gangs are mentioned in Hong Kong, they are typically linked to Triad societies (a kind of Chinese "heritage").There are some 40 triad organizations with over 40,000 members (Ho, 1985). However, the number of youth gangs is not as accountable because they exist everywhere where there are young people, including public housing estates, schools, commercial centres, sitting-out areas, parks, football pitches and basketball grounds (Luk, 2002). Several studies have been conducted in Hong Kong (CSWCYISC, 1999; HKFYG, 1993; Lee et al., 1996/97; Lo, 1984, 1992 & 1993). Some common findings show they exist in groups with a core-fringe structure, and share Triad subcultures with varying degrees of delinquency. Youth gangs involved in less serious delinquency (e.g. shop-theft, blackmail for small sums, vandalism, etc.), are regarded as at-risk youth who need special attention and are of high intervention priority. Without proper intervention or services, they run a higher risk of being further influenced by Triads, and consequently heightening the severity of their delinquent acts. Ultimately they may end up as hard-core criminals. Luk (2002) pointed out that the "righteousness" and "brotherhood spirit" once strongly emphasized in Triad societies have long disappeared. Triads are now mainly concerned about monetary gains and rewards through illegal means. Groups of young people (youth gangs), who join or are affiliated with these societies, can easily be influenced by the subculture and commit serious criminal acts.

Young Substance Abusers

As there is a trend for young abusers to take multiple substances at a time, it is quite difficult for officials now to identify what kinds of substances they have abused. Ecstasy has now been identified as one of the most abused substances, with nearly 200 different kinds available on the market. There were 2,049 reported young substance abusers under the age of 21 in the first half of 2000 (January-June), a 42.1% increase from 1,442 in the second half of 1999 (July-December), according to data provided by the Central Registry of Drug Abuse (CRDA). And there was an increase of 55.9% (from 700 to 1,091) newly reported young abuser cases in 1999 (Narcotics Division, 2000). "About half of the reported young abusers were within the age bracket 16–18" (Narcotics Division, 2000:6). Another report from the CRDA indicates that compared to the same period (January to June) in 2000, there was an increase of 24.7% reported young abusers (under age 21) in 2001; and newly reported young abuser cases also increased by 43.0% (Narcotics Division, 2001). Again, "about half (49.5%) of the reported young abusers were within the age bracket 16–18" (Narcotics Division, 2001:6). Ketamine and Ecstasy remain the most commonly abused substances by young people (Narcotics Division, 2002). It must be noted that there is significant under-reporting in this area so the actual number of young abusers is expected to be higher. Reports have revealed that discos and rave parties are popular occasions for young people to abuse illegal substances, and tighter substance abuse legislation for young people is needed (AOSWT, EDOSWT, SCOSWT & CWDOSWT, 2000; *Oriental Daily*, 16.7.2000; *Shing Pao*, 27.8.2000; *Sing Tao*, 27.8.2000 and *Sun Pao*, 27.8.2000). Unruly behaviour, such as promiscuity and gang fights are reported to be common among young substance abusers at discos and rave parties (*Oriental Daily*, 31.7.2000 and *Shing Pao*, 27.8.2000 and *Sun*, 27.8.2000). Through these observed cases, it is obvious that young people who abuse substances deserve our attention.

School Bullies

Although bullying among school students is not a new phenomenon, the fact that some students are persistently rejected, harassed and physically hurt by other students has drawn much public attention and concern (*Oriental Daily*, 1997; *Hong Kong Standard*, 1998; *Ming Pao*, 1999; *Sing Tao*, 2001). Bullying occurs where there is an imbalance in power between people, and it is a repeated or continued behaviour (Olweus, 1994; Smith and Sharp, 1994; Rigby, 1996). There is evidence that continued or severe bullying can contribute to problems of neurosis, sleeping difficulties, study difficulties, truancy and depression as well as long-term problems such as permanent anxiety, low self-esteem, school dropouts, delinquency and suicide (Sharp and Thompson, 1991; Olweus, 1993 & 1994; Smith and Sharp, 1994; Hugh-Jones and Smith, 1999). A more comprehensive local study on secondary teachers' and students' perceptions of school bullying in local districts was conducted in 2001 (Wong and Lo, 2001). Another community-wide research report on the prevalence of school bullying in primary schools in Hong Kong was also published in October 2001 (Wong et al., 2001). These studies reveal the severity of the problem among students in Hong Kong and this deserves our attention and intervention.

Young Delinquents

The last YAR group to be introduced in this chapter is young delinquents in Hong Kong. As shown from police statistics, the number of young people under the age of 21 that have been arrested between 1998 to 2000 contributed about 30% of the total arrested population, with 29.3% (12,447) in 1998, 30.7% (12,524) in 1999 and 31.0% (12,694) in 2000. (Commissioner of Police, 1999, 2000 & 2001). It can be observed that both the number of young arrests and the percentage are increasing steadily, so the situation deserves attention. Of the different categories of crime committed, "Shop-Theft" remains the most frequently committed offence. In 1998, there were 2,782 young persons arrested for the offence; and in 1999 and 2000, the number was respectively 2,433 and 2,451 (Commissioner of Police, 1999, 2000 & 2001). As juvenile delinquency has been a concern for society, the government has commissioned a study to explore the possible causes and solutions (Vagg et al., 1995). The study suggested that the problems that exist within different systems, including law enforcement, have caused an increasing number of juvenile delinquents. The study proposed the development of more measures to dispose at-risk young people so they do not enter the criminal justice system pre-maturely (Vagg et al., 1995). Other studies (Au, 1997 and Cheung, 1997) have indicated that the external social systems, e.g. family, school, peer groups and media, are also causes for deviance.

Overall, it can be concluded that the exhibition of different kinds of behavioural problems, e.g. hanging out with gangs, abusing substances, dropping out of schools and committing delinquency, are indicators of the at-risk situation of young people. They are actually signals for help and assistance. If appropriate help and assistance can be offered to these YAR and we can shift their energy to positive and constructive focuses from negative and destructive ones, these young people would have unlimited potential in our society.

After introducing different service programmes currently available to YAR in the next chapter, concepts and methods on how best to work with YAR with different behavioural exhibitions will follow.

2

Service Programmes for "Youth-at-Risk" in Hong Kong

Francis Wing-lin Lee

The destructive power of young people had caught the government's attention by the mid-1960s after a series of youth riots, which demonstrated how destabilizing a force youth power could be on society (Commission of Inquiry, 1967). By the late 1970s, the delinquent behaviours of young people had become so alarming that it led to the formation of a working group by the government to investigate the problem (Working Group on Juvenile Crime, 1981). In fact, the problem of juvenile delinquency in Hong Kong has been a big concern for the government, with the latest official commissioned research on the phenomenon in the early 1990s, and a published report in 1995 (Vagg et al., 1995). Because of its disturbing effect on society, the government has put much emphasis on handling the problem of juvenile crime. A few years ago, the government commissioned a study on the effectiveness of different rehabilitation programmes for young offenders (Lo et al., 1997). But it should be noted that the problem of "youth-at-risk" was not part of the government's priorities until a report on young night-drifters, a form of "youth-at-risk" (YAR) was released (Lee and Tang, 1999). The Secretary of Health and Welfare then stressed the problem had become part of the government's top agenda (*Ming Pao*, 29.5.2000). In early 2001, the Social Welfare Department announced that "Care for the Youth-at-Risk" would be the main theme of forthcoming youth services. In the new millennium, the development of youth services would follow the trend of integration of all disciplines, with youth-at-risk and juvenile delinquents considered top priorities.

Service Programmes for Youth-at-risk in Hong Kong

Ideally, before presenting different service programmes for YAR, the policy on YAR should be discussed first. However, it is regrettable that there is no such thing as an overall policy for YAR in Hong Kong. Policy-makers believe that different YAR service programmes already have their own policies so there is no need to have a separate policy to address YAR specifically. At-risk youth are, to a large extent, not official delinquents whose wrong-doings need to be punished under the legal system. They fall under the social welfare services who attempt to fulfill their developmental needs. To have an overview of different service programmes for at-risk youth, it is best to refer to the Five Year Plan for Social Welfare Development in Hong Kong published bi-annually by the Social Welfare Department.

According to the Five Year Plan for Social Welfare Development in Hong Kong (SWD, 1998), there are six service programmes that target youth-at-risk in different groups. They are: 1. Outreaching Social Work service, 2. School Social Work service, 3. Integrated Teams, 4. Community Support Service Scheme, 5. Hotline Service for Youth at Risk, and 6. Outreaching Social Work Service for Young Night Drifters (SWD, 1998). In fact, several services for YAR exist in the territory. These will be introduced in this chapter.

Outreaching Social Work Service

Outreaching Social Work (OSW) service is run by some non-governmental organizations subvented by the government. Through the use of casework, groupwork, mass programmes and activities, it aims to provide guidance services to individuals and groups of street youth (youth-at-risk) who are detached from conventional social systems (e.g. family and school) and hang around in groups in public premises such as street corners, parks, football fields, video game centres, billiard rooms and fast food shops, etc. (Coordinating Committee on Outreaching Social Work Service, 1989). The ultimate goal is to help these young people regain more sociable life styles. These young people, who do not normally participate in conventional social or youth activities, and who usually have a Triad background, are vulnerable to undesirable influences. They have created much public nuisance to the local communities and are in need of social work service. Historically, in a full OSW team, ten professionally trained social workers are allocated to a priority area where the service need is identified. As of March 2000, there were 34 OSW teams, serving in 34 priority areas/communities with relatively higher juvenile crime rate, and unserved youth population in the territory (SWD, 2000). "Outreaching social work aims to establish contact with these young people in the places they are known to frequent, ... and to provide counselling, guidance and other forms of service to help them overcome their problems, develop their potential and become socially reintegrated" (SWD, 1998:51). A geographically-based Integrated Team (IT) mode of service has been developed to meet the changing needs of children and youth. At-risk youth identified in the community are also served by the ITs. (For more detail on ITs, please refer to the relevant section below.) The establishment of OSW in the territory has to be changed. After some re-arrangement of the service districts and organizations, in September 2002, 16 Youth Outreaching Teams (YOTs), that work basically the same as OSW teams before, were formed to serve identified at-risk youth and street gangs in 16 priority districts in the territory (SWD, 2002).

School Social Work Service

School Social Work (SSW) service is provided to students in secondary schools. A social worker is usually attached to a secondary school, and provides individual and group counselling and guidance services to students. Most SSW services are provided by non-governmental organizations (NGOs) but the SWD also has a school social work unit with a few workers who deliver direct service to some secondary schools. In September 2002, there was one school social worker in every one of the 468 secondary schools in Hong Kong. Casework, groupwork and mass programmes/activities are employed in the service delivery process. The service aims "to identify and help students whose academic, social and emotional development is at risk. It seeks to assist them to solve their personal problems and to make maximum use of their educational opportunities and prepare them for adulthood" (SWD, 1998:51).

Integrated Teams/Integrated Children and Youth Service Centres

After conducting a two-year evaluation of children and youth centre services, a report published in 1994 recommended the service delivery model of integrated team (IT) for children and youth services (Working Party on Review of Children and Youth Centre Services, 1994). This model has become a development trend for the provision of children and youth services in the territory. For a standard full team, an IT would have 13 social work staff to service a youth population of 12,000. The IT model basically draws manpower from a child and youth centre, OSW and SSW, while some teams also have a Family Life Education Officer (FLEO). One of the IT's advantages is its flexibility to deploy resources to form sub-teams and employ different working approaches, e.g. reaching-out, attachment to school, centre-based, etc., to serve the indigenous young people with reference to their life/behavioural patterns. At-risk youth form part of the 12,000 youth population, and consequently, they also fall under the team's service target. At the end of June 2003, there were 130 ITs/ICYSCs (Integrated Children and Youth Service Centres in the territory (HWFB/SWD, 2003). There should be around 133 ITs/ICYSCs (Integrated Children and Youth Service Centres in the territory in 2003–2004 (HWFB/SWD, 2003). "With the flexibility in deploying the manpower and other resources pooled, and through adopting different service models and approaches, integrated teams can, ideally, effectively meet young people's multifarious needs and, at the same time, be responsive to community demand" (SWD, 1998:50).

Community Support Service Scheme

This Community Support Service Scheme (CSSS) was also recommended by the Working Party on Review of Children and Youth Centre Services (1994). The Scheme aims to help children and youth who have infringed the law or on the verge of law infringement to re-integrate into society. Counselling, structured supportive group programmes and intensive supervised activities are provided by the Scheme to supplement the existing casework and youth services for marginal youth (YAR) and young delinquent (SWD, 1998). In October 1994, the SWD started to subvent a CSSS project — Project Phoenix — of the Methodist Centre as a two-year pilot project (Lo, 1998). At the same time, the SWD also ran two units of CSSS at Kowloon East and Kowloon West for young probationers and subvented the Hong Kong Federation of Youth Groups (HKFYG) to run another unit of CSSS — Youth Support Scheme — at New Territories West. All these CSSS units were the review targets of an evaluation research (Lo et al., 1997). After the review, all units became long-term subvented schemes. Non-governmental organization (NGOs) schemes target young delinquents who have been cautioned by the police (Police Superintendent Discretion Scheme – PSDS), while SWD-run units target young probationers. In April 2000 the Project Phoenix agreed to confine the service targets who receive PSDS and live in the Hong Kong Island region (Methodist Centre, 2000). In 2001, three more units of CSSS run by 3 NGOs were set up in the territory. They are attached to the Tai Wo Integrated Team of the Evangelical Lutheran Church Social Service (serving Shatin, Tai Po/North & Yuen Long); Tsz King Integrated Team of the Hong Kong Playground Association (serving Wong Tai Sin/Sai Kung & Kwun Tong); and Cheung Sha Wan Integrated Team of the Boys' and Girls' Association of Hong Kong (serving Yau Tsim Mong, Kowloon City & Sham Shui Po).

Hotline Service for Youth-at-Risk

Since August 1995, SWD has subvented the HKFYG to run a hotline service for youth-at-risk in order "to provide hotline service for youngsters to call for help and advice instead of pending up their negative emotions leading to desperate acts, ... to prevent youth suicide by offering timely intervention through counselling" (SWD, 1998:52). An NGO, the Youth Outreach, also runs a 24-hour hotline for young people without subvention (Youth Outreach, 2001).

Outreaching Social Work Service for Young Night Drifters

A study commissioned by SWD to Lee and Tang (1999) on Young Night Drifters (YNDs) in the territory estimated that there were more than 10,000 YNDs who are at-risk of undesirable influences of various kinds, and are drifting in open space locations at night. Some 35–55% of them have service demands (Lee and Tang, 1999). With reference to the report, 18 night-shift OSW teams run by 13 NGOs, with the subvention of the SWD, especially targeting the YNDs have been set up in different districts in the territory. Their jobs include offering tangible assistance (e.g. escorting home) and referral, counselling and guidance services to the YNDs. Without subvention, Youth Outreach has been operating its own night outreach team with the support of two crisis centers since 1991 (Youth Outreach, 2001). However, with government subvention since July 2002, it now operates an overnight centre — The Hangout — for young people.

Working Group on Services for Youth at Risk

In the Five Year Plan, the Working Group on Services for Youth At Risk has been recognized as a kind of youth-at-risk service (SWD, 1998). This Working Group in fact has an advisory role and is not involved in any direct service delivery. The Group is formed to identify and examine major issues relating to young people. Recommendations to the government on the handling methods of different issues of youth-at-risk are made by the Group.

District Coordinated Projects

There are also projects at the district-level that are involved with different organizations, both governmental and non-governmental, to provide services to youth-at-risk. These district-based projects have adopted a multi-disciplinary approach and cooperation to serve the youth-at-risk at the district-level. Examples of these projects are Youth Action Network in Shumshuipo, Project Headway in Shatin, Community Youth Enhancement Scheme in Tai Po, Project Polar Star in Yuen Long, Project "X" in Tuen Mun, Scout Teams in Eastern District and Shatin, and so on. These projects basically have the involvement of some youth service organizations (of NGOs), the police, social welfare and schools. Through referrals, some identified at-risk youth are introduced to relevant services or activities for guidance purposes.

Understanding Adolescents Project

With government backing, the Understanding Adolescents Project (UAP) is now running in some primary and secondary schools following two years of experimentation in 11 schools in Shatin. The project is of a primary preventive nature. The purposes of UAP are for early identification and intervention of youth-at-risk in the school setting. Through the use of a set of screening tools (questionnaire), the youth-at-risk are identified. Different relevant service programmes, both at individual and group levels, are provided to these young people by social workers affiliated with the schools in order to direct them on to the right track.

Hostel Service

The Youth Outreach provides short-term hostel service to young people who have run away from home or who are temporarily unable to return home. It has two "crisis centres", one for boys and another for girls. Services in the centres basically include case and group counselling, school and career guidance and recreational activities (Youth Outreach website). Another NGO, the Hong Kong Student Aid Society, also runs three hostels for young people who, for various reasons, cannot live with their families and require accommodation.

Police Superintendent's Discretion Scheme

Although the Scheme is for juvenile offenders who admit to minor crimes, these juveniles can still be regarded as "at-risk" at the top level — "at-risk category activity" (McWhirter et al., 1998) as mentioned in the previous chapter. The Scheme can be regarded as a diversion measure "that seeks to avoid formal processing of the offender by the criminal justice system" (Clear and Dammer, 2000:27). This Scheme provides power of "a police officer of or above the rank of superintendent to issue a caution to a juvenile offender (under 18 at the time of caution) rather than initiate a criminal prosecution" (HKPF, 1995). There are some prerequisites that the police officer needs to observe before deciding on the cautioning. These are: 1. there is sufficient support for prosecution which is the only alternative, 2. the juvenile voluntarily and unequivocally admits the offence, and 3. the juvenile and his or her parent/guardian agree to the cautioning (HKPF, 1995). Upon the officer's decision, the case can be referred to the Juvenile Protection Section of the Force for follow-up visits for a period of up to two years or until the eighteenth birthday of the juvenile. Upon the consent of the juvenile's parent/guardian, the case can also be referred to the SWD or Education Department (ED) for relevant services (HKPF, 1995).

The programmes introduced above are some main services for YAR in Hong Kong. At a glance, it seems that Hong Kong has quite a number of service programmes for this group of young people in different forms and with various approaches. The effectiveness and adequacy of these different service programmes for YAR will be discussed in a later chapter (Chapter 8). However, one thing is certain. "Care for the Youth-at-Risk" has been designated as the main development theme for youth services in the coming years, and further service programmes and diverse forms and approaches will emerge.

3

Working with Youth Gangs: An RGC Approach*

Francis Wing-lin Lee

Youth gangs are usually of a neighbourhood basis (Cartwright, 1975; Cooper, 1967; Klein, 1971; Lo, 1992; Spergel, 1995). They are identified as having "anti-social", "delinquent", "violent" and "at-risk" natures (Cartwright, 1975; Feldman, 1985; Goldstein and Huff, 1993; Klein, 1971, Lee et al., 1996/97 Spergel, 1965). They exist well before detach workers intend to intervene in their daily activities. Most youth gangs have already developed into certain group stages and detach workers have to spend some time to explore and understand that stage before they can intervene. Also, most of these groups will still exist after the workers end their services with them. All the characteristics of youth gangs show that working with these groups demands the use of some unique methods.

In fact there is literature introducing the general principles and methods for working with unattached youth groups and street gangs (Collins and Hoggarth, 1977; Editorial Committee on Outreach Journal, 1985; Feldman, 1985; Goetschius and Tash, 1967; Klein, 1971; Lee, 1994; Lo, 1992; MacDonald, 1980; Morse, 1965; Spergel, 1965 & 1995). There are also accounts of different intervention methods for different groups of young people at risk and juvenile delinquents (Casey and Cantor, 1983; Cooper, 1967; Fashimpar and Harris, 1987; Goetschius and Huff, 1993; Li, 1990; Marks, 1977; Pawlak and Vassil, 1980; Pollio, 1995; Smith et. al., 1972; Witt and Crompton, 1996). However, all this literature is either too general in suggesting some basic working

---

* This article has been slightly revised from the article "Working with Natural Groups of Youth-at-risk: An RGC Approach" in Vol. 12(3) of the GROUPWORK Journal and that permission has been obtained from the Journal to reproduce the article.

principles or too specific in deliberating special theories. There is a need to develop an approach that can be commonly adopted for providing some concrete guidelines for working with youth gangs.

This study aims to investigate the working methods and common approaches that outreaching (OR) social workers (detach youth workers) employ in working with youth gangs in Hong Kong. By analysing the findings, factors that are significant for effective intervention in youth gangs are identified. Furthermore, an RGC Approach, which may provide some guidelines for intervention in youth gangs, is proposed.

Outreaching Social Work Service

Outreaching Social Work Service in Hong Kong, run by some non-governmental organizations but funded by the government, commenced in late 1979. This is a kind of youth service that provides guidance services to the street youth who are detached from conventional social systems (e.g. family and school), and hang around in groups in public premises such as street corners, parks, football fields, video game centres, billiard rooms and fast food shops. These young people, who usually have Triad backgrounds and are referred to as youth gangs, have created much public nuisance (e.g. vandalising, bullying each other) in the local communities, and have been assessed to be in need of social work service. Luk (2002) has identified the existence of four types of youth gangs: gangs in public housing estates, gangs in schools, gangs in commercial areas, and gangs in parks or open playgrounds. For a full outreaching social work team, ten professionally trained social workers are allocated in a priority area where the service need has been identified.[1] The primary aim of the service is to provide counselling and guidance to individuals and groups (gangs) of these young people so as to assist them in regaining pro-social life styles.

Methods of Study

In this study, two research methods were employed. First, copies of a pre-set questionnaire were sent to all OR social workers in 30 OR teams in the territory[2] for collecting information and opinions on working with youth gangs. At the time of the study, these teams had been serving in the prioritized communities for more than one year. The content of the questionnaire included: (1) their personal particulars, (2) their experience of working with youth gangs, (3) the skills used in working with this type of group, (4) factors they considered crucial for successful/ effective intervention with youth gangs and (5) factors they considered influential for unsuccessful/ineffective intervention with youth gangs. Ultimately, 153 completed questionnaires were returned. This response rate is quite satisfactory: 64.8% of all OR workers working in the 30 teams. Second, in-depth individual interviews were conducted with 19 experienced OR workers (K01–K19), each from a different OR team with a minimum of three years service.[3] The purpose of these interviews was to collect more qualitative data of their working experience with both successful and less successful cases of youth gangs.

General Profile of Youth Gangs

First, it is worth introducing some general characteristics of the youth gangs with whom OR workers have been working so that their context can be better understood.

Based on the information provided by the workers in the study, the average number of youth gang members ranged from five to eight. These groups/gangs of young people were predominantly male. In gangs of mixed gender, males usually out-numbered females and were more dominant. The female members usually had an inferior and subordinate status. When workers first started to contact and work with the gangs, the members were mostly in their early teens (13 to 15). Triad affiliation was quite common among youth gangs. Congruent with the literature (Cartwright, 1975; Lee et al., 1996/97; Thrasher, 1927), the structure of these youth gangs had three basic stratas: central leader(s), core members and fringe members.

Factors for Effective Intervention in Youth Gangs

The findings suggest several identified factors, which were considered as facilitative for effective intervention[4] in youth gangs.

Understanding of Gangs' Culture

All worker respondents pointed out that understanding the culture/ subculture of the youth gangs is fundamental for effective intervention in the gangs. This understanding includes knowing their beliefs and values, how they react to different things (attitudes) and how they talk and behave (behaviours).

Duration

A majority of the workers (132 or 86.3%) reported that the most effective time to intervene in youth gangs is between one to three years. This time frame is relatively long, so this means workers have to be patient to do this type of work.

Number of Group Members

Among the 100 workers who thought that the size of the youth gangs influenced the effectiveness of the intervention, most (76, 76%) said that the optimum number of gang members should be four to six; that is, a small group. As reported previously, the average size of the youth gangs that most workers had been working with was between five and eight. It seems the size of the youth gangs most workers had been working with was appropriate.

Level of Intervention

Among the three strata identified in youth gangs, most workers thought that working with the central strata (leaders and core members) of the gangs was an effective intervention method. The leaders and core members were, respectively, the most favoured first and second chosen levels of intervention.

Factors Crucial for Effective Intervention

When workers were asked to indicate the most crucial factors for effective intervention in youth gangs, "worker's relationship with the gang" was the most important (146, 95.4%). "Worker's understanding of the group dynamics of the gang" was the second most frequently chosen factor (101, 66.0%). "Crisis occurred in the gang for intervention" (70, 45.8%) and "worker's use of methods/skills" (67, 43.8%) were respectively in the third and fourth positions. So, "worker's relationship with the gang" stood out to be the most important factor for effective intervention in youth gangs.

Quality of the Worker

As a helping agent working mostly in natural settings, such as street corners and parks, the quality of the worker is especially essential for effective intervention work with youth gangs. Through the analysis of data, three areas concerning the part of the "worker" will be discussed: knowledge, skills and personality.

1. Knowledge

When asked to indicate what areas the OR service needs to improve on, a majority of workers thought that *"strengthening acquisition of working theories"* (91, 59.5%) would be an important improvement in the service for enhancing the effectiveness of their intervention work. Also, as disclosed in the above presentation, there is a need for workers to equip themselves with knowledge in such areas as small group theories, developmental characteristics, the needs of adolescents and Triad/gang's subculture and norms so that their intervention work can be facilitated. Some comments from the "experienced OR workers" (workers with more than three-year working experience in the OR service) support this observation:

> "I think the OR service should develop its own working theories so that workers can have more references for their practice." (K02)

> "I have to admit that my lack of concepts in working with youth gangs is one of my weaknesses." (K11)

> "I agree that I am experience-based. The context of your daily work is demanding and there is not enough literature in the field that you can refer to for assisting your work." (K15)

> "What can you do when you have lots of groups and gangs to handle? You can find no books and theories to help. So you have to depend on your own intuitions." (K19)

2. Skills

"Strengthening workers' working methods/skills" was the most frequently chosen answer for improvement in the OR service (132, 86.3%). As the daily demand of working with youth gangs grows pressing, equipping workers with appropriate working methods and skills is of utmost importance. Furthermore, as revealed from the above discussion, "the ability of workers to build up a good relationship with the youth gangs" was considered most crucial for effective intervention. As the ability of relationship building with youth gangs can be learnt as methods or skills, this further confirms the importance of studying the appropriate working methods and skills of OR workers in their work context. From the records of individual interviews with the "experienced

OR workers", it can be observed that the working methods and skills of the workers were favourable and had contributed positively to the intervention in the gangs. The workers' programming and organizing skills (e.g. in football, basketball, table-tennis, billiards, camping, hiking, canoeing) were often described as facilitative for relationship building with the gangs. The skills to reduce intra- and inter-gang conflicts, neutralize gang negative norms, promote democratic decisions in the gangs, de-group/de-gang, and so on, were demonstrated as effective methods of working with youth gangs. All these indicate that equipping workers with different working methods and skills is significant for effective intervention in youth gangs.

3.   Personality

From analysing the records of individual interviews with the 19 "experienced OR workers", several personality characteristics have been identified. These personality traits are believed to be significant for effective work with the individuals and group as a whole. They include:

Initiative: Approaching the gangs proactively and without reservation

Easy-going: Friendly and pleasant manners in interacting with the individual members as well as different subgroups of the gangs

Open: Being honest and truthful in communicating with the gang members

Accepting: Being free from biases and prejudice and not easily making judgement on the members

Patient: Allowing time for the working relationship to build up and being calm and in control when facing uncertainties

Alert: Being sensitive to the changes in the gangs and the environment for making appropriate intervention plans

Flexible: Can adjust and adapt to the changes in the social and physical environments of the gangs

Willing to learn: Can put down the "professional" mask and be humble enough to acquire new knowledge from the young people

Possession of the above personality characteristics would be beneficial for working with both individuals and groups.

Working with Youth Gangs — The RGC Approach

Group transformation (assisting a youth gang, which is a natural group of young people on the streets, and transforming into a more formal group with introduced structure such as football group) and de-grouping (deliberately facilitating the disorganization of the youth gang when its delinquent elements are out of control) have been proposed as methods for working with youth gangs in Hong Kong (Lo, 1992). However, not all youth gangs suit the criteria of using these working methods. For example, de-grouping should not be used for gangs that do not have strong delinquent tendencies; and for gangs that do not have proper common sports or recreational interests, group transformation could not be employed.

Based on analysing the findings of the present study, an RGC Approach, believed to be able to facilitate the intervention in youth gangs, has been proposed. The main aim of developing this approach is to offer some guidelines for detach youth workers while working with youth gangs on the streets.

The RGC Approach

The configuration of the RGC Approach is similar to that of the Process Model (Garland et. al., 1973) of social group work. It also stresses the understanding of the general group/gang phenomena at different stages of its development. However, the RGC Approach further highlights what intervention work needs to be done at different stages of intervention.

In this Approach, "**R**" stands for "**Rapport Building**", "**G**" stands for "**Group Focus**" and "**C**" stands for "**Case in Group**". "**R**", "**G**" and "**C**" are in working sequence and priority. That is, the detach workers should focus on "R" in the first instance when they start to work with a youth gang. When "R" is fulfilled to a satisfactory degree, they then can proceed to "G" as the work focus with the gang. Finally, "C" would be the main purpose of the intervention. In the following sections, the focuses and methods of work at different stages of intervention will be discussed. A case example, which is based on the information from the interviews with the "experienced OR workers" will also be presented in each section as an illustration.

"R"

As indicated from the findings of the present study, establishing and maintaining a trusting relationship with members of the youth gangs is a crucial factor for facilitating effective intervention. This Approach suggests that for working with the youth gangs, building up a trusting rapport with the gangs is of utmost importance and of first priority. Not only building a trusting rapport in the first instance, but maintaining a trusting rapport with the gangs and their members all through the intervention process is also essential. There are several methods and skills that can be used for building up an initial, then trusting relationship with the gangs in their natural settings.

Having short but frequent and casual contact with a youth gang at their own "base" (turf) is one method. Through this method, the presence of the detach workers on the spot can be gradually accepted by the gang. Participating in the activities of the gang, for example, through ball games, playing chess and chatting, is another method to be employed. However, workers should be cautious about not engaging in illegal activities, such as gambling or gang negotiations. Providing assistance to the gang as a whole or individual members when they are in crises is another possible method. Examples of crises are when they are being interrogated by the police in their "base" or when they are being complained about by the neighbours for being a nuisance or vandals in the community. If workers can successfully "save" the gang from these problems, their relationship with the gang can be positively promoted. Furthermore, if workers know that individual gang members are in crises, such as being expelled from school or sacked, having conflicts with the family or being arrested, helping these individual members to face or resolve the problems by providing appropriate assistance is also a useful method for building up a trusting rapport with them. It is believed that with dynamic interpersonal skills together with the preferred personality characteristics discussed above, the "R" stage of intervention in a youth gang can be completed satisfactorily.

Case Illustration

This was a gang of five boys aged twelve to fifteen who used to gather in a football field in a public housing estate. They were studying in either secondary 1 or secondary 2 and were schoolmates. Since all their parents had to work in the day-time, they were not supervised. Their academic performance was poor. Neighbours complained that they bullied their children who played in the field and broke their windows with footballs. When the worker received the information, he carried out several sessions of field observation on the gang at the spot (football field). He gradually established contact with the gang by casually, but purposefully joining their football activities. He introduced himself to the boys as a youth worker in the community who helped organize different youth activities. Through the contact, he had become more familiar with the personality of different members as well as their dynamics in the gang. The members had also started to accept him as an acquaintance. About two months after the initial contact, during one session when the worker went to the field to meet the boys, they all looked anxious and upset. It was because three of them had been involved in an assaulting event in school and were suspended for a week. They did not know how to tell their parents and were afraid that they would be expelled from school. In this crisis, the worker first helped them ventilate their anxiety and also made them realize their wrong-doing. The worker encouraged them to face the reality and accompanied the three boys home to tell their parents about the event. With the worker's intervention, even though their parents were very angry with the boys, they finally forgave their sons. The worker also contacted the school principal and discussed the case of the boys. Finally, the principal agreed to allow the boys to resume schooling three days later, but they had to promise not to break the school regulations anymore. After the incident, the relationship between the worker and the gang greatly improved, and the image of the worker as a capable helping agent was established.

"G"

When the pre-requisite of rapport building has been fulfilled, the intervention focus can move forward to a "group focus". At this stage, the workers should explore common legal interests of the gang members and try to provide or organize group activities or programmes which are of interest or are exciting for the gang members, such as football matches, camping wild, canoeing, rock climbing and adventure voyages. The use of such programmes has several advantages. It can divert the energy of the members in a more healthy way. The image of the workers as resourceful people can be further enhanced. Through organizing the programmes, more information of the members can be collected (e.g. through filling in of registration forms), while their unique characteristics and problems can be better understood (e.g. through more formal contact). Guidance to the gang, to some extent, can also be provided. Last but not least, the relationship of the worker with individual gang members can be further promoted. This is the stage for the full use of the programming skills of the workers.

However, it should be remembered that the size of the group engaged in activities or programmes should be manageable—that is the group should be small. Otherwise, the process of the activities or programmes cannot be supervised adequately. As discussed above, a youth gang with four to six members is appropriate for intervention by the workers. Providing group activities or programmes to different subgroups of the gang, if it is relatively large, can also be considered. Trying to limit the number of participants in a programme by setting a quota is another method that can be used for group reduction. This quota setting method is in fact a kind of structuring of the youth gang and hence the "natural" nature of the gang will be reduced.

Case Illustration

After six months of contact with a gang of seven youngsters aged fifteen to eighteen who had Triad affiliation and used to gather in a corner of a residential block in a public housing estate, the worker had built up a trusting relationship with the gang. The worker discovered that although they used to boast about their abilities in doing everything, most of them had never gone camping before. So the worker decided to organize such an activity for them in order to help them develop their interest. The gang agreed to join the event and thought that it was an easy job. During the camping process, the members began to realize their lack of knowledge and skills in wild life such as hiking skills, reading maps, setting tents and cooking in the wild. Although the camping activity was a painful experience for most of them, some had actually developed an interest to learn more about wild life. Since the worker was quite knowledgeable on camping activities, his image as a capable youth worker was established among the gang. Through this activity, the worker also discovered the potentials of some members who had good leadership ability. Aside from helping some members develop their interest, these activities helped the worker to forge a closer working relationship with individual members.

"C"

Once stage "G" of gang intervention has been carried out for some time and the image of the workers as helping agents has been gradually established, the intervention can proceed to stage "C". As mentioned above, the primary goal of intervention in youth gangs in the Outreaching Social Work Service is to provide guidance to youngsters in these groupings so that they can regain pro-social life styles. So after a certain period of group focus work, and when the rapport between the worker and the group (gang) as well as individual members has been further developed and maintained, it is time for more individual guidance work — that is "case in group" work. Although the gang is composed of different members who seem to share some common values, attitudes, behaviours and norms, they are in fact unique individuals with their own unique problems, strengths and weaknesses. "Case in group" focus means doing casework in a group context. That is, through the gang (a kind of group), workers can identify different individuals at-risk and offer them appropriate guidance according to their unique situations and needs. Although individual guidance, which is the defined service objective of Outreaching Social Work, is the main focus at the "C" stage, the merits of providing guidance to these young people through the use of groups should not be neglected. When the workers can successfully work with different individual members of the youth gang, their intervention work can then be considered effective.

As presented above, the level of intervention that most workers saw as effective for intervention in the youth gangs was the central strata; that is, the leaders and the core members. Klein (1971) has suggested that intervention work with youth gangs should focus on a small number of gang members by suggesting the existence of the group effect in youth gangs. He stated that "when a detached worker worked with a small number of gang members, there would be indirect influence on the whole gang" (Klein, 1971: 163). So with limited time and energy, workers can focus their individual guidance work with gang members in the central strata in order to make their intervention more effective.

Case Illustration

This was a gang with four boys and two girls aged between fourteen to sixteen. The gang was initially contacted in a video game centre but they later shifted their gathering places to fast food shops and a small park in the community. The worker had been working with this gang of young people for about two years. Through organizing different activities and programmes for the gang, such as barbecues, outings, camping wild and visits to amusement parks, the worker finally managed to invite them to work as volunteers in a carnival organized by the team. Through this period of intervention, the worker gradually built up a trusting and helping relationship with different members. She had also become familiar with the personality of and problems faced by different members. She had helped two boys find new schools when they were expelled. She had assisted a girl, who was an informal leader in the gang, to reconcile with her mother after some heated quarrels concerning her unstable work situation. She had also provided individual guidance to different members who had encountered problems with the opposite sex. In fact guidance both on an individual and group level was being offered.

Epilogue

Above is an account of the RGC Approach proposed for working with youth gangs. In fact at different stages of the intervention, different methods and skills have to be employed or developed by the concerned workers. The development and creation of relevant working methods and skills rely much on their practice wisdom. It should also be remembered that the time required for different stages of intervention in a youth gang will vary depending on its dynamics and situation and the intervention plan and skills of the workers. It is believed that with the appropriate knowledge, skills and personality, the effectiveness of employing this approach to work with a youth gang can be seen within two to three years' time — the period indicated by most workers for effective intervention with youth gangs.

The RGC Approach aims to provide some guidelines for promoting more effective intervention in youth gangs. The author acknowledges that it is still at an early stage. With conscious employment of this approach in working with youth gangs and the accumulation of the experience of using this approach, it is believed that the content of this approach could be further enriched.

4

Working with Young Substance Abusers:
A Harm Reduction Approach

Cecilia Wing-yin Ho

At the beginning of the twenty-first century, the drug/substance use scene in Hong Kong has been changing drastically, particularly with regards to young people. With the imported rave/disco and dance culture from the West, the number of young people taking Ecstasy (XTC) and Ketamine (K) has risen in the last few years. Taking Ecstasy has become just another weekend leisure activity for some young people and young adults. Without doubt, they do not fit into the stereotype of a traditional drug user taking heroin or cocaine.

Different social service agencies have put their focus on seeking an understanding about the drugs situation among adolescents and young adults, and exploring effective strategies to combat this new "war on drugs" as a response to the worsening situation (Caritas Aberdeen OSW Team, NAAC Eastern OSW Team, CYMCA Chai Wan OSW Team, HKPA WC/NP OSW Team, HKYWCA C&W OSW Team, 2000; Committee on Substance Abuse, HKCSS, 2000; HKCS, 2000; HKCSS, 2000; Outreaching Service, HKPA, 2000). These studies have shed light on related knowledge, but the importance of a public health approach — harm reduction — was not promoted. Young substance abusers are always portrayed as deviants. In fact, adolescent substance users construct meaning about their drug use within the context of interpersonal relationship which is deemed very crucial to them. In short, a critical approach to viewing substance use/abuse as a complex social issue with specific political implications rather than as an epidemiological concern (an individual disease, a psychiatric disorder or even an implicit moral failing) should be taken into account when working with young substance users/abusers (Ettorre, 1992). From frontline practice experience and Lee's report, new approaches must be sought to work with substance users in a disco environment as one of the general "way-outs" — the "Say No to Drugs" approach has proved to be unsuitable for occasional or recreational drug users (Lee, 2001). It is important to invest some effort on determining whether a locally defined harm reduction approach in working with young substance users/abusers can be found in Hong Kong.

Ecstasy

Ecstasy often named as "E", "Adam" or "XTC" is known chemically as Methlenedioxymethamphetamine, or MDMA for short. MDMA is produced synthetically in a laboratory from Methamphetamine. According to the Mersey Drugs Journal (Redhead, 1993), scientists developed MDMA while searching for an appetite suppressant for soldiers during the First World War. Thus, MDMA was not a new drug. It was patented in 1914 as an intermediary for more advanced therapeutic drugs. In 1985, MDMA was made a schedule 1 controlled substance in the USA, despite opposition from psychiatrists who had been using it as a therapeutic tool to reduce fear and promote acceptance, thereby facilitating communication (Rosenbaum, 2002b). MDMA was made popular in the late 1980s and early 1990s both in the UK and the USA.

Both in the West and in Hong Kong, discourse on drugs has made drugs a problem not the other way around (Redhead, 1993). To most people, MDMA has been associated with night clubs in various parts of the world, especially in western countries such as the USA and Britain with "Acid House", "rave" or "dance culture" music prevalent around the mid-1980s. There are many differences between the use of Ecstasy and that of other drugs such as heroin or cocaine. Most of those who use Ecstasy have good careers and qualifications, and don't come from broken families or have a low self-image. Indeed, they may also need to pay a lot of money to join rave parties.

New Trends in Substance Use — "Recreational Drugs"

In Hong Kong, the Finance Committee of the Legislative Council approved a grant of $350 million for setting up the Beat Drug Fund in March 1996 (ACAN, 2002). It aims at promoting anti-drug activities, which can help alleviate the problem of drug abuse, particularly among young people. For the general public in Hong Kong, there seems to be a universal consensus that we, as adults, need to prevent young people from using drugs. In addition, there is no debate over the potential therapeutic use of MDMA. However, for many people who like to go to raves and discos during the weekend, the pleasure of "E" far outstrips any potential dangers that the drug may possess. Substance use amongst young people in Hong Kong is so widespread that it can no longer be adequately explained by the traditional notion of deviance.

In Hong Kong, according to the Central Registry of Drug Abuse (CRDA), in the first quarter of 2004, the overall number of reported substance abusers showed a downtrend. However, the number of newly reported drug abusers aged under 21 showed a slight increase, from 421 in the first quarter of 2003 to 429 in the same period of 2004. (Hong Kong Narcotic Division, 2004). The most commonly abused drugs for young people under 21 were Ketamine (74.7.%), Ecstasy (34.1%) and cannabis (18.3%). Mostly, these abusers were reported to have abused psychotropic substances occasionally or at recreational venues such as discotheques (Hong Kong Narcotic Division, 2004).

Thus, drugs at raves have become a community and media concern. Responding to the alarming rise in the use of "recreational drugs" such as Ecstasy and Ketamine among young people in Hong Kong, the police force has searched almost every popular disco including rave parties in different districts in order to prevent teenagers from taking drugs or fooling around in these areas. Both the police, the press and even the general public have "moral panic" when youngsters dance in raves and/ or discos simply because the dancing culture is closely associated with drugs-taking behaviour (Ho, 2001).

Club Drugs in Hong Kong Context

Ecstasy is an outdoor drug which means that people are mostly taking it in discos/rave parties, and rarely at home or in a hidden way. Most teenagers in Hong Kong usually take drugs in a disco-setting. They are pills which can easily be digested. They do not need complex preparation unlike taking heroin or "ice". In fact, there is an interesting marketing approach to selling "E". For instance, its pill design is very attractive and ever-changing within a short period of time. Sometimes, its design helps signify which "producers" the pill has been sourced from. Both Ecstasy and Ketamine are weekend drugs, there is little evidence to show that ravers are using them during the week, or more specifically when not engaged in leisure pursuits. Most of them use the substances during "time-out" periods or when people are having vacations. Club drugs users always dissociate themselves from opiate drug users whom they see as "junkies". They call themselves "Ravers" instead. In addition, from the author's experience, club drugs use is now widespread amongst many social groups ranging from so-called youth-at-risk to elite professionals. There are differences in their drugs use patterns, their perspectives regarding its use, and even the venues.

Club drugs, especially Ecstasy, does not have many attendant symptoms as with other drugs. Users do not seem to suffer from many withdrawal symptoms. However, we cannot obtain an accurate data profile of drug users, especially those "E" and "K" users, from CRDA, the official statistical data on drug trend in Hong Kong. We can only take reference of the trend as shown on the CRDA data. Substances induced issues are complex and deserve more in-depth discussion. The greatest problem facing club drugs users is quality control. In a black market, the relationship between a vast amount of predominantly culturally "unsophisticated" users and dealers are continually open to all manners of exploitation and mistrust (Redhead, 1993).

Polarization of Drug Treatment Programmes in Hong Kong

Most of Hong Kong's Drug Treatment programmes target one of two population groups — abstainers or severe abusers. This sort of polarization reflects the polarized thinking behind the dominant discourse about substances — use equals abuse, zero tolerance or become a junkie/addict. There are no drug treatment programmes promoting moderate or responsible use in Hong Kong. In between the continuum of abstinence and addiction, there are also important levels of different substance use. They include experimentation, limiting dosage of substance use, infrequent use, occasional use or maintenance etc. However, these levels are generally ignored by most programmes and services in Hong Kong. Harm reductionists should help fill this gap.

What Is Harm Reduction?

Harm reduction is an umbrella term based on an international public health movement. It is a set of practical strategies that reduce negative consequences of drug/substance use, incorporate a spectrum of strategies from safer use, to managed use, to abstinence (Harm Reduction Coalition, 2001). It is very difficult to have a universal definition of or a formula for implementing harm reduction. However, its strategies should start where drug/substance users are, and address conditions of use along with the use itself.

The harm reduction movement should be viewed as a part of the human rights movement. According to the Harm Reduction Coalition website (2001), there are several principles central to the harm reduction practice. All these principles are in line with social justice, equality and human rights. Firstly, harm reduction accepts the fact that people do engage in high-risk behaviours such that licit and illicit drug/substance use is part of our world and we can choose to work to minimize its harmful effects rather than simply ignore or condemn them. Secondly, we should understand drug/substance use as a complex, multi-faceted phenomenon that includes a continuum of different levels of use from severe abuse to zero tolerance, and recognizes that there are some ways of drugs/substances use that are less harmful than others. Thirdly, harm reduction is to affirm drug/substance users themselves as the primary agents of reducing the harms of their drug/substance use, and seeks to empower them to share information and support each other in strategies which meet their actual situations of use. Lastly, to recognize that the realities of poverty, class, racism, social isolation, past trauma, sex-based discrimination and other social inequalities affect both peoples' vulnerability to and capacity for effectively dealing with drug-related harm (Harm Reduction Coalition, 2001).

There are lots of examples of harm reduction practices in society. Take sex education with the use of condoms for example. Unavoidably, many teenagers today still choose to have sex. From a harm reduction standpoint, it would be better to give teenagers information about sex, pregnancy, and STDs, and provide condoms to reduce the risk of STDs for those who choose to have sex. In this way, we are reducing the potential harms associated with sex. In addition, earplugs, seat belts, abortion and prostitution are examples of reducing harm no matter whether you like it or not. To uphold the principles of harm reduction, we should first, do no harm (Denning, 2000).

In the West, many mental health clinicians are searching for better treatment strategies for people who have drug problems (Denning, 2000). They recognize that in applying harm reduction principles in psychotherapy, it is important to work closely with the stated goals of the clients and to lower the threshold to allow higher accessibility of treatment. As mentioned before, there is no inevitable progression from use to dependence. Drug/substance users are an extremely heterogeneous group, and can range from one-time curiosity seekers to stable working people who use mind-altering substances to relax and enhance social interaction. Their experiences will have a diverse range of outcomes (Denning, 2000).

Scare Tactics Are Ineffective

Ecstasy and Ketamine are very unique because they are closely related to the rave/disco culture or the dancing context, generally regarded as normal leisure activities in most societies. It is quite different from people who use heroin, methamphetamine or many other drugs/ substances which are mostly used in private venues such as staircases of buildings. In a study, none of the female drug/substance using informants experienced any feelings of shame, guilt or disgrace that heroin-users or some traditional drug users might commonly feel (Ho, 2001). As Lee (2001) stated, Ecstasy and Ketamine challenge the classical concepts of addiction as there is no conclusive evidence showing physical dependence. Their use does not automatically lead to recognizable and confirmable physical and psychological problems (Lee, 2001). The National Institute on Drug Abuse (NIDA) in the U.S. hosted an international conference announcing the latest research breakthroughs on Ecstasy's physiological and psychological effects. There was no conclusive answer and it is crystal clear that more research about Ecstasy's long term effects on the brain is needed (Rosenbaum, 2002a). Indeed, researchers shared a lot on short term or immediate negative effects of overheating, dehydration, adulterated substances containing poisonous substitute chemicals in that conference. Most importantly, they advocated a realistic harm reduction media campaign to tackle the situation (Vastag, 2001).

In Hong Kong, there has been an upsurge in Ecstasy use during rave parties and discos. The Narcotic Division of the government has publicized a threatening advertisement linking Ecstasy with brain damage and death (ACAN, 2002). Although research of possible brain change, such as depletion of serotonin, associated with substance abuse exist, it is unacceptable to link each and every death to using Ecstasy. Such threatening tactics are not the most pragmatic way to approach MDMA-users who indeed use their bodies for experimental purposes. Most drug using people are aware of the potentially harmful effects and toxicity of Ecstasy and Ketamine. Most female drug users can share their subjective memory impairments induced by their club drugs use (Ho, 2001). However, such factual knowledge and negative experience of Ecstasy and Ketamine has not deterred them from continuing using. In addition, regardless of respondents' backgrounds, 35 out of 100 adults admitted taking Ecstasy was a positive experience, according to NIDA-funded research done shortly after criminalization of Ecstasy in 1987 in the U.S. (Rosenbaum, 2002a). They felt fulfillment in using MDMA in their lives. In Hong Kong, youngsters have no difficulty in getting Ecstasy in discos or rave parties. Some substance users who have gone through anti-drugs programmes are increasingly skeptical about the "just say no" approach.

In Hong Kong, the "drugs kill" or using "your brain on drugs" approach may be effective on those who have never had contact with drugs/substances. However, understanding that drug educators have an abstinence-only agenda, young people often ignore or take these messages lightly. The side-effect to this problem is that it creates a huge crisis of credibility. The government has poured lots of funding on the anti-Ecstasy campaign through disseminating warnings on the medical and legal aspects of getting involved in this drug/substance. Still, new comers join in and the existing ones continue.

Whenever I meet young disco-goers, I ask them about their perception of the government's warnings of possible brain damage. Those veterans express great cynicism. Even though they have experienced lots of negative consequences of taking XTC or Ketamine, they still continue to take them as they have no hope in the future. It is very difficult to help marginalized youth get a job in the current unfavourable economic situation so it seems that taking XTC or Ketamine is the "only" way they can feel in control of their lives. Many substance users laugh at the threatening messages generated by the scare tactics. For drug counselling and education, I think it is important to consider seriously about the client's unique relationship with each drug. Research (Zinberg, 1984) has identified the interaction effect between three factors — drug, set and setting — in the initiation and maintenance of controlled drug use. *Drug* refers to the actions or pharmacology of the drug itself, and it includes considerations of potency, route of administration, adulterants, and legality. *Set* describes the personality of the person using the drug, and it includes concepts such as risk taking, mood, motivation, expectancy and emotional state. *Setting* refers to the context of drug use, e.g. the venue and the people who use it. We can see that each drug user's experience is unique. Thus, it is useful to affirm drug users themselves as the primary agents of reducing the harms of their drug use, and seek to empower them to share information and support each other in meeting their real situation of using drugs/substances.

Youngsters Encounter Ecstasy (XTC) and Ketamine — Spectrum of Attractions

In my study which explored the conception and practice of drug use among female adolescents in rave parties and discos in Hong Kong (Ho, 2001), I found that there was a spectrum of attraction for youngsters to use both XTC and Ketamine. The following are some of the attractions my study found. XTC has stimulant effects — it increases self-confidence, raises one's energy level and gives people no mood to eat. XTC is available with prescription drugs and most drugs of abuse do not involve needle use (Inciardi et al., 1993).

> Female adolescents like to snort "K" because the "K" effects make them more feminine. Besides, "K" can make them "high" in a short period of time and it makes them feel dizzy and tired. Males always like to take care of those girls. For girls, it may be the most effective and "legitimate" way of flirting with boys inside discos. — A teenage female substance user

From the above quote, it can be seen that the female respondent played a role in shaping the so-called traditional notion of femininity. Through being taken care of by males, female adolescents can increase their self-value by taking advantage of being traditional females (i.e. to be dependent).

> XTC can help me dance energetically and feel competent. — A teenage female substance user
>
> You can dance more energetically after taking Ecstasy, and can hang on till the end of the party. — A teenage female substance user

The stimulant energetic effect is felt by the substance users in the above quote.

> You must eat less in order to be slim and have body shape, which let you dance more attractively on the dance floor. Taking Ecstasy can help you do that. — A teenage female substance user

XTC can suppress one's appetite. Teenage females like to be on diets and are particularly concerned about their body shape. They would like to lose weight and see positive reasons in continually using XTC.

It is safe to take "E" or "K" in rave parties as they are in a pill-form ("E") or powder-form ("K"). Whenever the police come, we can flush them away. — A teenage female substance user

"E" and "K" are easy to dispose of since they are in pill or powder form. This has increased the attractiveness of the drug for adult consumption.

Practice of Harm Reduction

Using substances assertively as a way of mastering oneself can be a kind of self-directed activity (Ettorre, 1992). Teenagers sometimes "choose" to take drugs as part of their life activities. It would be unwise to give up perspectives to understand drug/substance use as a social and/or individual problem. We can still have an alternative understanding of viewing drug/substance use as a leisure or pleasure pursuit. This consideration could be very useful for understanding the picture of drug/substance use in which services and policies have to be well addressed. We should consider a more "user-friendly" approach which moves beyond stereotypes and encompasses the active participation of teenagers in reducing the harms from their drug/substance use (Ho, 2001). An effective drug education scheme should be designed to save lives and reduce health problems, rather than mere propaganda about total abstinence, which might not be the choice of all individuals (Rosenbaum, 2002a).

Negative reactions to MDMA have been the result of "fake" Ecstasy use, according to much research (Holland, 2001). Dancesafe — a harm reduction organization aiming to minimize risk in the dance community — indicates that as much as 40% of their tested "Ecstasy" pills were not MDMA. Instead, they contained substances such as PMA (paramethoxyamphetamine) and DXM (dextromethorphan — an active ingredient in Robitussin cough syrup) (Holland, 2001). In Hong Kong, we do not have any organizations helping with pill-testing. It is impossible for the users to know the ingredients. The substances are in a black and unregulated market. No quality control is one issue; while genuine information is another issue. We, as drug educators, sometimes get the latest news developments of the drug scene from newspapers and magazines which might often be infotainment-oriented rather than knowledge-based. It should be the duty of the Narcotics Division to update us on the trends of the drug scene and the ecology (patterns and concepts) of the people who use/abuse them. This can be done through web-sites and education seminars (Lee, 2001).

Apart from controlling the influx of drugs to Hong Kong, it is important to keep down the cases of morbidity and mortality associated with drug/substance use in parties and discos (Lee, 2001). Many teenagers are concerned about the harmful effects and toxicity of club drugs. Teenagers have their own "street-wise" precautions such as drinking Chinese medicine/herb (after taking XTC or Ketamine) in order to detoxify. In fact, whenever I share some harm reduction thoughts with teenagers I meet inside discos, and they show lots of interest in finding out how to avoid complications. Therefore, providing them with harm reduction educational materials is important.

Research findings have suggested that the rapid onset of diminishing and/or punishing returns associated with drugs use would discourage long-term abuse (Beck and Rosenbaum, 1994). Therefore, drug education should target speeding up drug/substance users' diminishing returns and increasing their life opportunities. It is crucial to use and share adolescents' experiences to help them re-think their drug resistance/reception process—what does drug resistance/reception mean? (Freedman and Combs, 1996). One thing that needs to be emphasized is that some people need drugs in their lives for their own lifestyle or culture's sake.

I do not want to be fixed in either demonism or romanticism about drugs scene as postmodern thought suggests us to look at specific, contextualized details more often than grand generalization, difference rather than similarity. Echoed in the above statement, the process of examining cultures of drug/substance use is also crucial. Not only does it have implications for perspectives on drug/substance use, and in turn their effect on policy and practice, it can also give us specific targets and appropriate media for harm reduction. In Britain, harm reduction messages addressing the "dance drug" phenomenon have targeted popular culture that could be very successful if awareness of drugs within this culture is taken as a guideline (Redhead, 1993). However, harm reduction is still not very well accepted by the general public in Hong Kong. Thus, "say no to drugs" is still the dominant discourse or propaganda in Hong Kong's drug education.

Some drugs overdose prevention practices include the provision of well-lit chilling down areas and free drinking water so dehydration can be reduced as this is an immediate side effect of taking XTC. These "save lives" measures should be disseminated to youths.

Saying "know" to drugs that emphasizes a balanced view of drug knowledge (both positive and negative sides) is better than encouraging youths to say "no" to drugs. Obviously, Hong Kong's harm reduction movement still has a long way to go. However, drug educators should take up this responsibility to move forward. The quality of life and well-being form the main criteria for measuring success of drug education not the downtrend of the consumption of drugs/substances.

More research should be done to observe the interactive and ever-changing nature of various pharmacological, psychological and sociological factors with a client-led mentality on drug/substance use. The continual challenge is to make sense of this dynamic interplay which exists among drug, set and setting.

5

Strategies for Tackling School Bullying:
A Whole-School Approach

Dennis Sing-wing Wong and Sindy Sin-ting Lee

Bullying among school pupils is not a new phenomenon. The fact that some pupils are persistently rejected, harassed and physically hurt by other pupils has been described in mass media as well as in literature. In Hong Kong, there has been a growing concern about the violent and bullying behaviour of students in the media.[1] In 1997, a boy was tortured to death and the corpse was burned as a result of group bullying.[2] In 1999, a teenage girl was sexually harassed by a group of her classmates on the stairs of a housing estate near the school.[3] Recently, a boy hurt his classmate with a chopping knife in class after being verbally bullied for several months.[4]

Bullying is seen as repeated oppression, physical or mental, of a less powerful person by a more powerful person or group of persons. It occurs where there is an imbalance in power between people, and it is a repeated or continued behaviour (Olweus, 1994; Rigby, 1996; Smith & Sharp, 1994). There is considerable evidence now that continued or severe bullying can contribute to immediate problems such as neurosis, sleeping difficulties, study difficulties, truancy and depression as well as long-term problems such as permanent anxiety, low self-esteem and dropping out of school. The worst outcome is that a severely bullied child takes his or her own life (Hugh-Jones & Smith, 1999; Olweus, 1993; 1994; Sharp & Thompson, 1994a; Smith & Sharp, 1994). School bullying has been identified as a major problem in many countries around the world (McCarthy et al., 1996; Perry et al., 1988; Rigby, 1996; Tattum & Tattum, 1996; Whitney et al., 1994). Discussion and guidance on dealing with victims started emerging in the late 1980s.

It is important that school bullying is stopped within schools or else it may create a vicious cycle of school violence. This chapter highlights research and findings of some local studies related to school bullying. We will discuss some common strategies for tackling the problem of school bullying. We will, in particular, present an anti-bullying programme, which has been undertaken in a secondary school recently. This programme has adopted a "Whole-School Approach".[5]

Research in Bullying

Although there are some isolated studies of bullying before the 1970s, systematic studies of the phenomenon started from the late 1970s (Smith & Sharp, 1994; Smith et al., 1999). In 1978, Dan Olweus published an English version of his book, *Aggression in the Schools: Bullies and Whipping Boys* (originally published in 1973 in Swedish). It marked the opening of a stream of research on bullying, which developed first in the Scandinavian countries. From a survey of more than 130,000 Norwegian students, Olweus found that some 15% of the students in elementary and secondary/junior high schools in Norway were involved with bullying problems (as bullies or victims) with some regularity. Analyses of teachers' feedback in approximately 90 classes confirmed that the survey results did not give an exaggerated picture of the prevalence of the problem in Norwegian schools. It really affected a very large number of students (Olweus, 1993).

With growing international interest in, and concern with, the problem of bullying, researchers have focused on various aspects of the social phenomenon including the incidence and nature (Besag, 1989; Olweus, 1978, 1994; Rigby, 1996; Smith et al., 1999; Tattum, 1993); characteristics of victims (Olweus, 1978; 1994; Rigby, 1996; 1999); attitudes towards and perceptions of bullying (Boulton, 1996; Rigby, 1996; Siann et al., 1994); the effects of bullying (Hugh-Jones & Smith, 1999); the views of teachers (Byrne, 1999; Olweus, 1978; 1994; Stephenson & Smith, 1989); bullying in schools and the development of criminality among others (Farrington, 1993; Baldry & Farrington, 2000); and reactions to bullying (Arora, 1994; Cowie & Sharp, 1994; Elliott, 1997; Smith & Thompson, 1991). A number of researchers (Harachi et al., 1999; Mellor, 1999; Smith, 1999; Smith & Sharp, 1994) have noted that school bullying has not been recognized as a problem of concern in the United States and in the UK until fairly recently.

In Hong Kong, there was no systemic study on school bullying before 1999. In the past two decades, what can be identified as relevant to the issue of bullying are studies on causes or predictors of delinquency (Cheung & Ng, 1988; Vagg et al., 1995; Wong, 2001a); the nature and extent of youth deviant behaviours in local districts (Chow et al., 1985; Law, 1986; Wong et al., 1995); the process of deviation (Wong, 1998; Wong, 1999a; 1999b; Wong et al., 1995); and the unruly and delinquent behaviours of pupils (Education Department, 1991; 1993). Since mid-2000, Wong (Aberdeen Caritas Outreaching Team & Wong, 2000; Wong, 2001b; 2001c) began investigating teachers' and students' perceptions of school bullying in local districts as well as on a community-wide level. For instance, the results of the first comprehensive research on secondary school teachers' and students' perceptions of bullying were published in mid-2001. The study collected 905 questionnaires from teachers and social workers, and 3,297 questionnaires from students, from 29 secondary schools (Wong & Lo, 2001). Another community-wide research report on the prevalence of school bullying in primary schools in Hong Kong was also published in October 2001 (Wong et al., 2001). Altogether 7,025 questionnaires were collected from 47 primary schools. These studies found that more than two-thirds of students were involved in the bullying problem — either as bystanders, bullies or victims (see Table 1).

A Quest for a Comprehensive Intervention Strategy

To combat the problem of school bullying, the Ministry of Education in Norway initiated the first nationwide campaign against bullying in 1983. A large range of media such as journals, booklets, videotapes for illustrating the effects of bullying, and ways for handling it, were produced for related professionals. In connection with the campaign, a large-scale longitudinal study was conducted in Bergen and Norway. Around 2,500 students were followed over 2.5 years. The results showed that there was a 50% decrease in the rate of bullying over two years after the campaign started. Thereafter, two other national programs were undertaken in 1996 and 2000, respectively. A booklet for teachers on the use of general management approach to improve social interaction in class and cooperation with parents was published in 1996. The Ministry of Education also established a nation-wide network for relevant professionals, and developed a central body for resolving bullying and other behavioral problems of students in 2000 (Arora, 1994; Roland, 2000)

Table 1   The Prevalence of Primary and Secondary School
Bullying Problem in Hong Kong

	Secondary School (%)*				Primary School (%)#			
	Physical Bullying	Verbal Bullying	Exclusive Bullying	Bullying with Extortion	Physical Bullying	Verbal Bullying	Exclusive Bullying	Bullying with Extortion
By-stander	58.6	87.7	72.7	34.3	67.6	87.4	65.6	40.2
Bully	17.2	45.5	22.6	6.6	22.5	52.1	24.4	9.5
Victim	18.3	46.9	17.6	8	31.7	61.9	28.1	13.2

*   The study collected 3,297 students' questionnaires from 29 secondary schools in 2001.
\#   The study collected 7,025 students' questionnaires from 47 primary schools.
N.B.   Percentages in the table represent the number of respondents involved in bullying over the past six months at the time of interviewing.

From the 1970s onwards, psychologist Bob van der Meer in the Netherlands began advocating policies to tackle the problem of bullying as described by Limper (2000). He wrote a number of books and articles, gave talks in schools, trained school counsellors, and provided counselling services to the victims' families as well. However, he failed to evoke a positive response from the government. It was not until 1992, when researcher Ton Mooij, concluded his first study on bullying, that it emerged there were 385,000 children (25% of primary school population) bullied in schools (quoted in Limper, 2000: 126). Since then, the "National Education Protocol Against Bullying" in the Netherlands began. Elements of this Protocol include:

- Social skills training for bullies and victims;
- Providing information to teachers and parents on causes of bullying;
- Actively informing pupils of the existence and extent of the problem;
- Appointing confidential counsellors in schools;
- Working closely with schools and encourage sharing of experiences; and
- Signing a "Protocol" to fight against bullying.

Parents organizations have also paid attention to the problem of bullying. They publish articles regularly, offer packages to parents, and produce puppet shows for school pupils. Based on the Olweus questionnaire, Mooij developed a "bullying test" and students can indicate the extent of bullying through the computer. Teachers could use the test results in the classroom for discussion. As a result, bullying is now on the social agenda in the Netherlands. A number of countries including Italy, Austria, Belgium, Denmark and Norway have already joined in this project (Limper, 2000).

Anti-bullying Programmes in Hong Kong

There has been no comprehensive intervention strategy developed to deal with the problem of school bullying in Hong Kong. Governmental or non-governmental bodies in Hong Kong have never published any educational package for combating the problem. A recent survey of teachers' perceptions towards school bullying in secondary schools showed that over 80% of respondents opined that the following anti-bullying programmes, which are commonly adopted in other countries, have never been organized in their schools (Wong & Lo, 2001). These programmes include:

- Anti-bullying seminars or workshops for parents;
- Early-intervention and self-protection programmes for potential victims of bullying;
- Anti-bullying curricula and law-related education curricula for students;
- Peace education courses for students;
- Aggression reduction and anger management programmes for students.

It is apparent that not many schools in Hong Kong are aware of the use of a whole-school approach to tackle or prevent the problem of bullying despite the fact that there have been numerous discussions in this area all over the world (Arora, 1994; Limper, 2000; Ortega & Lera, 2000; Peterson & Rigby, 1999; Roland, 2000; Salmivalli, 1999; Sharp, 1996; Sharp & Thompson, 1994a). The study of Wong & Lo (2001) also confirms that programmes in assisting teachers and parents to deal with the problem of school bullying are rare in Hong Kong. When respondents in their study (N=905) were asked to think of some possible solutions for preventing school bullying, they suggested the following methods:

- Lowering down teacher-student ratio in class (88.2%);
- Organizing joint programmes between school and social service agency in school (75.3%);
- Providing training to teachers to handle the problem of school bullying (68.8%);
- Having a long-term whole school anti-bullying strategy (58.0%); and
- Organizing teachers-parents cooperation projects (52.4%).

So far, no formal policy has been made by the Education Department to take the school bullying problem seriously. Yet, a number of voluntary social service agencies are willing to join hands together to implement programmes to raise awareness of the negative effects of bullying on the district level. Some have been working closely to develop packages for tackling the problem since 2000. Among these programmes, we will focus on discussing one anti-bullying programme which adopts the whole-school approach.

Here we share some important anti-bullying programmes in different countries (see Table 2). Apparently, a comprehensive anti-bullying programme, which includes cooperation among all parties in school and covers a wide range of activities, is important for prevention as well as tackling school bullying. The following are some common elements that anti-bullying programmes in schools should consist of:

Element 1:   Have a set of long-term anti-bullying strategies and procedures

Element 2:   Train teachers and parents in handling school bullying

Element 3:   Provide social skills and emotional control training packages to students

Element 4:   Adopt a multi-disciplinary cooperation strategy

Element 5:   Involve students to resolve conflicts

Element 6:   Conduct survey or test to monitor the situation

A Whole-school Approach: The Theoretical Framework

It is generally believed that a whole-school approach should be adopted to tackle the problem of bullying in schools (Arora, 1994; Humm & Mocroft, 2001; Rogers, 1995). To enable implementation of the anti-bullying policy, the school authority should define procedures and programmes for preventing and treating bullying behaviours. The theoretical underpinning of a whole-school approach is team-building and communication theories. All parties concerned should work hand in hand to define policies and procedures for dealing with cases of bullying. When they are implemented, changes will need to be made to accommodate unforeseen circumstances and dynamics in a short period of time (Sharp and Thompson, 1994b). Thus, it is important to maintain good communications among all parties, including parents, teachers, social workers and students. A whole-school approach can be implemented at a number of levels. To allow readers to have a clear concept of the whole-school approach, based on the model suggested by Sharp and Thompson (1994b: 24), we have constructed the following framework for intervention (Figure 1).

Table 2 Summary of Recent Anti-bullying Programmes in the World

Year	Authors	Country		Effectiveness
1994	Arora, C.M.J.	UK	• Focus on bullying as part of an integrated whole school policy • Acknowledgement of bullying as a social process • Clarity of communication • Involvement by the staff in developing the survey method • Emphasis on involvement of parents in a variety of ways • Making the first intake feel at home • A culture of "it's OK to tell" • Involvement of outside agencies	Unknown
1999	Salmivalli, C.	Finland	• General awareness-raising, self-reflection and rehearsal • Assertiveness training: not only for the victims • Structural intervention: re-networking the class • Use of peer counselling • Use of peer helpers in role-play • Choosing good peer helpers	Unknown
1999	Peterson, L., & Rigby, K.	Australia	• Encouraging students' participation in anti-bullying action • Setting up the anti-bullying committee • Setting up peer helper group • Setting up public speaking group • Setting up poster group and drama group	• Reduce bullying in the first year • Peer victimization is lowered
2000	Ortega, R., & Lera, M. J.	Andalucia (S. Spain)	The Seville anti-bullying in school project : • A programme for the management of school life • Use of cooperative group work and the curriculum • A programme for learning: The emotional, attitudinal, and value dimension	• Bullying is being opened • The victims can seek help more easily • The bullies end up being deprived of the passive support

(Table 2 to be continued)

(Table 2 continued)

			The Andalucian project: • Distributing leaflets • Setting up a telephone "help line" • Conducting a survey • Circulating a book about bullying	• The witness can reject the passive role
2000	O' Moore, M.	Ireland	• Training of teachers • Creating a school ethos • Ensuring comprehensive and monitoring measures • Developing procedures for reporting, investigating and dealing • Developing support programs for bullies and victims • Working with local agencies	Unknown
2000	Roland, E.	Norway	• Publishing articles and booklets for head-teachers and teachers about bullying • Addressing bullies and support victims • Constructive resolution between bullies and victims • Communication with parents • Discussing the problem in class • Producing a videotape for teachers, parents and pupils illustrating bullying and discussing methods • Involving the mass media to recognize important points for effective implementation • Holding seminars for students • Establishing a nation wide network of local professionals to assist schools	• A 50% decrease in the rate of bullying after the campaign was started.

(Table 2 to be continued)

(Table 2 continued)

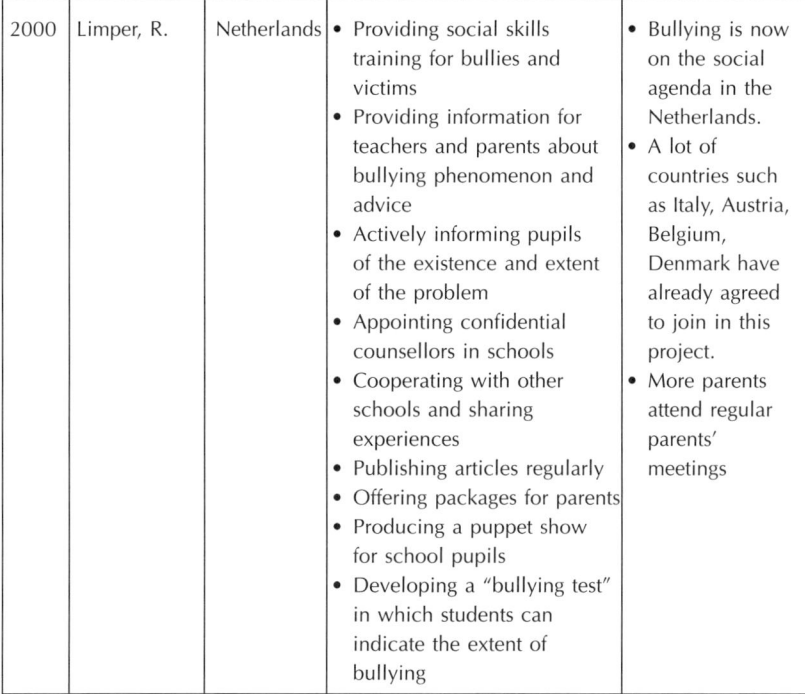

| 2000 | Limper, R. | Netherlands | • Providing social skills training for bullies and victims
• Providing information for teachers and parents about bullying phenomenon and advice
• Actively informing pupils of the existence and extent of the problem
• Appointing confidential counsellors in schools
• Cooperating with other schools and sharing experiences
• Publishing articles regularly
• Offering packages for parents
• Producing a puppet show for school pupils
• Developing a "bullying test" in which students can indicate the extent of bullying | • Bullying is now on the social agenda in the Netherlands.
• A lot of countries such as Italy, Austria, Belgium, Denmark have already agreed to join in this project.
• More parents attend regular parents' meetings |

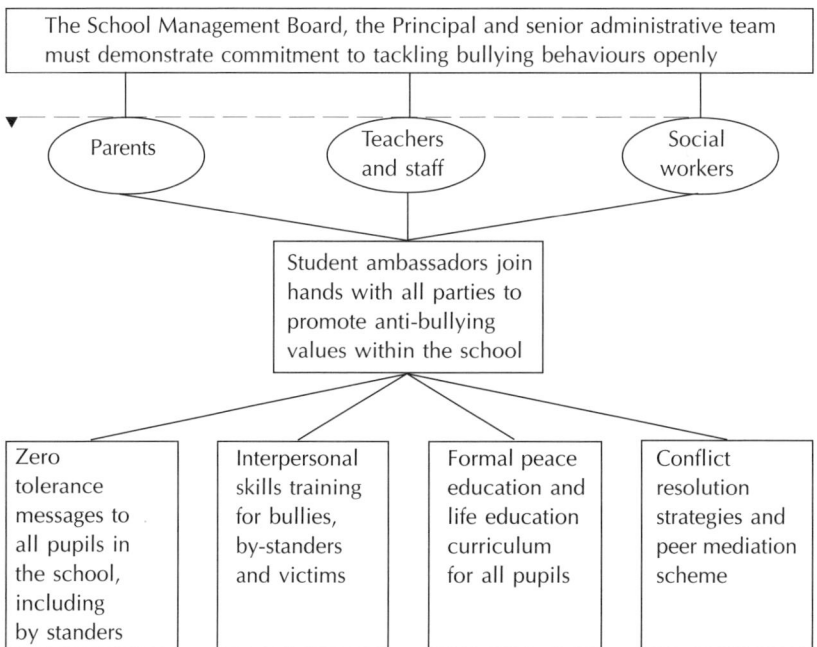

The School Management Board, the Principal and senior administrative team must demonstrate commitment to tackling bullying behaviours openly

Parents

Teachers and staff

Social workers

Student ambassadors join hands with all parties to promote anti-bullying values within the school

Zero tolerance messages to all pupils in the school, including by standers

Interpersonal skills training for bullies, by-standers and victims

Formal peace education and life education curriculum for all pupils

Conflict resolution strategies and peer mediation scheme

Figure 1 A Framework of Whole-School Approach in Tackling Bullying

A Pilot Anti-bullying Programme in Hong Kong — A Whole-School Approach

Based on the practice wisdom of many countries (Arora, 1994; Bodine & Crawford, 1998; Elliott, 1997; Glover et al., 1998), we initiated the first comprehensive anti-bullying programme in Hong Kong from August 2000 to April 2001. In this period, we worked with teachers of the school and a team of social workers from the Centre of Restoring Human Relationships[6] to promote a harmonious and loving environment in a secondary school. The objective of this project was to create a peaceful and happy learning culture among students, to decrease the number of bullying incidents, and to enhance students' intra-personal as well as inter-personal skills. This pioneer programme only targeted the junior form students (Secondary 1 to Secondary 3), and was funded by the government's Quality Education Fund.

With reference to the six elements of a whole-school approach mentioned previously, we firstly organized a series of activities for the participation of parents. At the beginning of the academic year, our team made good use of the orientation weeks to provide training to parents regarding prevalence and causes of bullying. We publicly invited parents to join the anti-bullying movement and to confront and prevent the problem of bullying assertively. Apart from mini-lectures, some social workers taught parents about good communication skills, and shared with them ways of building a rapport between parents and children through role-play and skills demonstration. Through these talks, the school is educating parents by telling them it takes bullying very seriously, and that it would contact the parents of children involved in bullying .

In the second month, we organized a staff development day for the school principal, teachers and social worker staff of the school. We shared with all parties concerned some recent overseas and local research findings on bullying, and the systematic ways for preventing and tackling bullying. During this training workshop, a clear message was passed to the teachers: "Bullying can grow to become very serious or it can be nipped in the bud" (Sullivan, 2000). If teachers know of bullying or suspect that it was occurring, they should deal with it in a systematic manner. At the end of the workshop, participants were asked to plan policies and procedures for counselling bullies, assisting victims and educating bystanders in their school. They were also encouraged to run a series of peace education curriculums for students (Table 3).

Table 3   Session Themes and Objectives of the Peace Education Curricula

Session	Themes	Objectives
1.	Introduction	• Introduction • Norms setting • Ice-breaking
2.	Self-understanding	• Recognizing personality and individual uniqueness
3.		• Understanding the existence of emotions • Familiarizing with different emotional states • Knowing emotional behavior
4.	Emotion	• Knowing about how to express and control emotion
5.	Control, Anger management & Mid-term Evaluation	• Knowing about how to be a congruent individual • Learning the relationship between emotion and action
6.		• Understanding the belief system of human beings • Teaching skills in anger management • Reflecting what we have learnt
7.		• Knowing about perception • Learning creativity • Knowing steps for solving problems
8.	Problem Solving Skill	• Learning how to set goals for problem-solving • Understanding EQ and problem solving abilities
9.		• Exploring priority of values • Learning inter-personal communication skills
10.	Positive values	• Knowing relationships between values and society
11.		• Teaching listening and concentration skills
12.	Inter-personal Communication Skill	• Teaching verbal expression and presentation skills
13.		• Enhancing non-verbal communication skills • Learning active listening skills
14.	Conclusion & Final Evaluation	• Understanding life challenges • Evaluating the effectiveness

After the staff development day, the school authority decided to set aside a 90-minute lesson each week to run a peace education course for all secondary one, two and three students. The course would be fitted in during the regular formal curriculum. This means each student would receive a total of 21 hours of peace education in the academic year, the first ever one to be conducted in Hong Kong.

As shown in Table 3, the programme consists of four major parts such as self-understanding, emotional control, problem-solving skills, and inter-personal communication skills. To maintain quality of the course, we organized a number of pre- and post- course planning meetings with all class-teachers from secondary one, two and three classes.

Effects of Cooperative Efforts

To actively help students participating in the course, different techniques and methods such as structural experienced games, worksheets, role-play, group discussion, video shows, debates and competition, were employed. With the help of these methods, most of the students could stay alert in classes and pay attention to messages that were shared. Unlike formal and tedious traditional classroom teaching, we encouraged opinion sharing and pupils' active contribution throughout the whole course. Social workers involved in the training were reminded to adopt positive discipline techniques, which emphasized exploration and encouragement but not punishment. Overall, they worked in partnership with students. Most of the learning activities were student-driven. Social workers mainly played the role of facilitators.

To collect systematic feedback from students, we distributed two sets of evaluation questionnaires to the students. One was for mid-term evaluation, and the other for the final evaluation. Results of the final evaluation suggested that over 80% of the participants (N=640) highly appreciated the curriculum's design and social workers' attitudes. About 75% of students found that this peace education course was innovative and valuable. During the evaluation meetings with the school principal and teachers, we noticed that opinions from most of the teaching professionals were positive. Most of the teachers said students became more confident in expressing opinions and innovative ideas in class. Students' emotional state was relatively stable after attending the peace education course. Students seemed to have learned self-discipline, and conflicts between teachers and students greatly decreased. The vice-principal opined that some of the troubled students began to have greater concern for others' feelings, while their inter-personal communication skills also improved a lot. The principal's opinion was very positive too. He pointed out that most of the students had developed a better sense of belonging, and cases of bullying decreased sharply. All these results and observations seem to suggest that the objectives of the whole-school programme, had to a great extent, been reached.

This pilot project tried to cater to all six elements of a whole-school anti-bullying programme mentioned previously. Firstly, the school authority openly agreed a long-term anti-bullying strategy. Secondly, all concerned parties such as the principal, teachers, parents and students were targeted and motivated to join in. Thirdly, a multi-disciplinary cooperation approach was adopted. Teachers worked closely with university professors as well as social workers to tackle bullying. Fourthly, students were involved in designing and implementing the programme. Fifthly, the peace education curriculum definitely trained up students' social skills and approaches to anger management. Sixthly, evaluation surveys were conducted to monitor the progress and effects of the programme. Since no previous similar programmes have been conducted in Hong Kong before, there was no base-line for comparison. It should be noted that, upon completion, all parties including teachers, parents and students felt the programme should be continued in the coming years.

Conclusion

We would like to share some final remarks that we have found. Firstly, we are glad that the present whole-school project was a pioneer and successful one. The project's programme content was in line with the one adopted in the UK (Arora, 1994). Apart from teachers and parents, a total of 640 junior secondary school students received peace education courses during the six-month period.

Secondly, while we were working with a group of whole-hearted teachers, our observation was that these teachers were kind, but had inadequate knowledge in anti-bullying methods. They were rather ignorant in regards to skills in student counselling as well as strategies for tackling bullying such as the "No Blame Approach", "The Pikas Method of Shared Concern" or "Peer Mediation Tactics" (Sullivan, 2000). In the models adopted in Finland and Australia, the school authorities put great emphasis on the participation of students such as establishing support groups, providing intensive student training and holding regular educational mass programmes (Salmivalli, 1999; Peterson & Rigby, 1999). These are good examples for teachers in Hong Kong to consider.

Thirdly, teachers in Hong Kong tend to take up all the tasks by themselves but they seldom voluntarily seek help from social workers or other relevant professionals. The present programme has set a good example for teachers to show them how to work closely with social work professionals.

Fourthly, we discovered that the average size of the present peace education training class was about 35. In order to allow students' active participation, class size should be reduced to around 20.

Fifthly, it seems the implementation of the anti-bullying programme has neglected the education of bystanders and potential victims. For instance, we think that assertive training or self-protection programmes for potential victims are necessary.

Despite the fact that we have devoted much endeavour to run a whole-school programme, compared with the models adopted in Norway, Spain and Netherlands, our programme was only a tiny and localized one. In fact, there is no central mechanism to coordinate schools to tackle bullying at a community-wide level. In Hong Kong, we do not have adequate indigenous publications related to bullying. In addition, we rarely involve mass media in promoting attitudes of anti-bullying in schools and do not have any telephone hotlines for such a purpose (Limper, 2000; Ortega & Lera, 2000; Roland, 2000). Nonetheless, this whole-school project is an innovative and valuable attempt. It can at least set up a good example for discussion in the education field.

6

Police Diversion Measures for Juveniles at Risk

Karen A. Joe Laidler

Philosophy and Debates over Diversion

What is diversion? How does it work? Does it work? Although these questions seem simple enough, the answers are more complex and must be understood in particular historical, cultural and social contexts. At a broad level, diversion is a strategy designed to divert offenders from the criminal justice system. In some instances, it is used as a pre-arrest mechanism to keep offenders from officially entering the criminal justice system such that at the time of detection, the police do not pursue an arrest. Offenders can also be diverted after arrest, at the pre-trial stage, with the charges being "bound over", and dependent on the offender's ability to stay free of arrest for a specific period. Offenders may be diverted even later in the criminal justice process at the point prior to or after sentencing or even during release from an institutional sentence (Spooner et al., 2001).

Although the intent of diversion, at any point in the process, is to move offenders away from the criminal justice system, what precisely are they being diverted to? In some instances, offenders may simply be diverted away from the system with the hope that they will not get into trouble and get arrested again. This type of diversion involves handling the case informally through non-intervention or "doing nothing". This form of diversion is the dominant approach used in dealing with juveniles, as evidenced by police studies showing that only a small proportion of the cases coming to their attention result in arrest (Horwitz, 1995; Ezell, 1995). This approach is consistent with Schur's (1973) proposal of radical non-intervention.

However, in other cases, offenders are diverted to alternative community-based programmes, operated by a variety of agencies from the police to social welfare to community organizations. This is a second type of diversion, and has been the subject of much controversy and debate. On the one hand, advocates of this form of diversion argue that these alternative programmes can address offenders' presenting problems in a non-stigmatizing and less formal manner, and consequently, reduce the likelihood of labeling and further offending. In this way, diversion acts as a crime prevention strategy. On the other hand, critics perceive diversion can have unintended effects, and become yet another mechanism for organizing and controlling offenders but in a non-custodial environment. From this standpoint, the offender who agrees to being diverted, is still under official, albeit less formal control, and is subject to a number of rules and conditions. If any of these rules are violated or the offender does not comply with the diversion programme, he or she can wind up being processed through the formal system on the original charges. This possibility raises other legal concerns about procedure and due process (Feld, 1999; Backes, 1995). Control agents counter argue that the implicit threat of formal processing is the major means of ensuring compliance with the diversion order. Yet, if the offender was simply released (as in the first form of diversion), he or she would avoid the justice system altogether.

Whether diversion should be administered by the juvenile justice system or by non-governmental agencies has also been at the center of debate (Ezell, 1995). Some observers argue that diversion programmes administered by agencies like the police run counter to the philosophy of diversion and its theoretical underpinnings in labeling theory. According to this view, diversion programmes operated by the juvenile justice system serve only to extend the reach of control agents. Instead, diversion is best operated by community agencies to avoid further contact with a formal system and thereby avoid stigmatization. Research however, has shown that juveniles who have been in diversion programmes have experienced labeling effects irrespective of its administration by the justice system or community agencies (Ezell, 1995).

This chapter looks first at the development, experiences, and controversies with diversion in the international context, particularly in the U.S. and the U.K. We then turn to examine the workings of diversion in the context of the juvenile justice system in Hong Kong.

The International Experience

During the 1960s and 1970s, policymakers, juvenile justice practitioners, and juvenile advocacy groups in several countries argued for reforms of their juvenile justice systems. The demands for reform were driven by a variety of factors, but particularly a growing dissatisfaction with the spiraling growth of juveniles in correctional custody without any demonstrable reduction in crime, a recognition of the ineffectiveness of individualized treatment in juvenile corrections, and a growing policy interest in the implications of labeling theory for juvenile justice.

In the U.S., the federal government passed the 1974 Juvenile Justice and Delinquency Prevention Act, mandating states to separate juveniles from adult jails, and to deinstitutionalize status offenders and minor delinquency cases from secure custody. It also encouraged states to develop diversionary programmes for juvenile offenders with the goal of reducing state dependency on secure confinement. The federal juvenile justice system made funding conditional upon compliance with the mandated components of the Act. In relation to diversion programmes, however, the federal government could only encourage rather than mandate states to set up alternative programmes to incarceration.

Although this juvenile justice policy was hailed as a landmark policy in the "best interests" of young people, evaluations of different components of the Act have shown its mixed success. Most states have complied with the separation of juveniles in custody from adults in jails, showing a dramatic decline in the number of young people in adult facilities. However, Austin, Johnson, and Gregoriou (2000) indicated a reversal of this trend with a recent rise in juveniles in adult custody, largely following the rise in the number of juveniles adjudicated as adults.

The deinstitutionalization of minor and status offenders and diversion programmes, however, has been the subject of much more heated debate. Although evaluations have shown a significant reduction in the number of young people being incarcerated for status offenses, there have been other processes at work that negate this decline. For example, although the number of status offender cases disposed of by the juvenile courts remained relatively stable from 1975 until 1985, it began to drop thereafter, but, as Schwartz (1995) had noted, this decrease had been absorbed by an increase in the number of delinquency cases being heard in the juvenile courts and a corresponding increase in admissions to public and private correctional institutions. Among the latter type of custody, Schwartz (1989) found that there has been a tremendous growth in the use of psychiatric facilities to "treat" troubled youngsters. In effect, the U.S. juvenile diversion movement resulted in the opposite of its original intent with the increase in "formal" options and the rise in custody rates. The reasons for the U.S. failure to realize true diversion may be partly attributable to the federal government's reliance on states' voluntary rather than mandatory participation to encourage diversion (Schwartz 1995).

With the passage of the 1969 Children and Young Persons Act in the U.K., the movement to divert young people away from the justice system began in earnest in the 1970s with the police, teachers and social workers forming juvenile liaison panels to review and decide on whether individual youngsters should be prosecuted or diverted from the system. The spirit of these multi-agency panels, rooted in the philosophical tenets of labeling theory, worked toward reducing the number of youngsters appearing in court. This collaborative scheme shifted the intervention emphasis from individualized casework to group work. Other cautioning schemes, largely controlled by the police, emerged during this period and have come to be the most widely used measures in dealing with youngsters today. While in the early 1970s, approximately one-third of youngsters under 17 years of age were cautioned, about 60 percent of juvenile offenders received a caution in the U.K in the 1990s. Like the U.S., some observers viewed the British cautioning scheme as a means for net widening with minor offenders, who could have simply been warned and released, being brought into the formal control system (Muncie, 1999). Questions have also been raised about "cautioning plus schemes" as offenders are required to make reparation but without any judicial process or protections. Critics also pointed to the strengthening of the criminal justice net as sentences meted out were disproportionately more severe than the offense.

In the 1980s, efforts in the U.K. to divert young offenders from secure custody gathered momentum with the passage of the 1982 Criminal Justice Act which introduced strict criteria in setting custodial sentences, requiring judges to justify the appropriateness of custody in all cases (Matthews, 1995). At the same time, the options for alternatives to custody grew such that a new type of diversion emerged, designed specifically for more serious offenders who were at a real risk of being incarcerated. Department of Health and Social Services moved on its initiative to develop intensive intermediate treatment growth of new diversion and community service orders. Although some observers were skeptical of these new developments, believing that the juvenile justice net would only continue to strengthen and expand with more options, the result was a reduction in both juvenile crime and in the number of young persons in custody. These changes have been linked to a number of factors, including a decline in the general youth population, the stringent policies on the recommendation and use of custody by social workers and the judiciary respectively, and the adoption of justice based diversion programmes that place the offense rather than the emotional needs of the offender at the center of treatment (Matthews, 1995; Muncie, 1999). With the expansion of the diversion strategy in the 1990s for more serious offenders and for the young adult population, some observers argued that the juvenile justice system was increasingly less concerned with welfare and justice and more oriented towards delinquency management or corporatism (Muncie, 1999).

At a broader level then, efforts to decarcerate and divert young people away from the juvenile justice system in the U.S. and the U.K. have led to a number of unintended consequences. In the U.S., critics challenged the justice system for widening its net — drawing in youngsters who would otherwise have been left alone, strengthening its net with greater levels of intervention, and diversifying its net by introducing new programmes without changing existing ones (Muncie, 1999). In the U.K., initial diversion schemes in the 1970s led to an increasing number of young persons being drawn into diversion, who would otherwise have been informally dealt with, and an increasing number of youth into being prosecuted who would have been better suited for diversion. Although observers feared similar problems with the criminal justice reforms of the 1980s, the 1990s witnessed a decline in the use of custody, but a rise in the use of justice oriented diversion programmes.

The Hong Kong Experience

What are the trends in the use of diversion in Hong Kong, given the experiences in the U.S. and the U.K? There are two main points of diversion. The first point can occur when the police come into contact with a young person whom they believe has violated the law and they may choose to warn the young person and make a note of the incident in their report book. This form of diversion, as noted in our earlier discussion, is a common practice in other countries. The police may instead bring the young person back to the police station for questioning and possible arrest. Checks are conducted to determine if the young person has a criminal history record, is a wanted person, or staying illegally in Hong Kong. If the police bring the young person (16 years of age or less) to the police station, a caution statement is taken from the young person in the presence of the parent(s) or guardian(s). If the young person is over the age of 16, he or she has the right to request the presence of legal counsel prior to giving the caution statement. A caution statement is a written account of the incident. The young person may be released if there does not appear to be enough evidence to prove the charges.

Alternatively, the police may charge the young person if there is sufficient evidence. At this point, the police review the juvenile's caution statement, the nature and severity of the offense; prior criminal history; and the attitude of the young person and his or her parent(s) or guardian(s). Having done this, the police will select an appropriate response. The officer in charge, who is at the rank of Superintendent or above, may exercise personal discretion to caution the juvenile providing that the juvenile has not yet turned 18 years of age and has admitted to the offense. The young person and his or her parent(s) or guardian(s) should also agree to the cautioning. As part of the police caution, the young person may be referred for services of the Social Welfare Department, Education Department and Community Support Services Scheme of an NGO, and may receive supervision and monitoring for up to two years or until his or her eighteenth birthday by the police's Juvenile Protection Services (JPS). The JPS supervision involves periodic home visits with the young person and his or her parents, discussion of school progress, leisure activities and peer relationships. The JPS officers also routinely contact the Social Welfare and Education Departments to review the juvenile's progress and problems with the family. Police are increasingly referring cautioned persons to the Community Support Services Scheme which offers a range of services to encourage young people to turn away from crime. These services include counselling and support groups, job training and placement, skills learning, outdoor activities, volunteer programmes, and programmes for parents and guardians (Fight Crime Committee, 1999).

This system, referred to as the Police Superintendent's Discretion Scheme (PSDS), started in 1963 and was restricted to young persons between the ages of 7 (the then minimum age of criminal responsibility) and 14 years of age. In 1995, the upper age limit was increased to 17 years of age. In that year, PSDS was also extended to include young offenders involved in non-opiate minor drug offenses with the proviso that this was their first offense and the quantity was small. These extensions were part of the government's larger reform to address juvenile crime (Provisional Legislative Council, 1997). In 2001, the Secretary for Justice organized a committee to review a possible extension of the diversion scheme to those persons between 18 to 20 years of age but this proposal was voted down. Arguments in favour of the extension included cost savings to the justice system, low recidivism rates, and the provision of after care services which might not be available through prosecution (Fight Crime Committee, 2002). The main counterargument centred on the legal definition of an adult. That is, persons 18 years or older are legally an adult, and therefore, must be held responsible for their adult actions. A similar proposal to extend the Scheme to adult offenders was unanimously defeated on the grounds that the Justice Department reserves control over criminal prosecutions, the existence of a range of sentencing options, including for minor offenses, and presumptions about adult accountability (Fight Crime Committee, 2002). In July 2003, the minimum age of criminal responsibility in Hong Kong has been moved up to 10, so the young persons to be considered for PSDS are now aged 10 to below 18.

The PSDS has, since its inception, been based on the philosophy of preventing the stigmatization of the young person and preventing further involvement in crime and the criminal justice system. Parents' participation is seen as critical to the young person's progress. The few available studies of Hong Kong's juvenile justice system suggest that this diversion scheme has contributed to an expansion of control over young persons, particularly those who have committed minor offenses. According to Gray (1996), the rise in juvenile arrests during the 1980s was matched by a significant increase in juvenile cautions, with the latter climbing from 89 to 340 per 100,000 between 1978 and 1989. On the surface, these corresponding increases suggested that diversion was operating to keep juveniles out of the system. However, closer examination of young persons continuing through the formal juvenile justice process throughout the 1980s indicated that the net was being widened and strengthened with juveniles who committed minor offenses and with one or no prior convictions being sentenced to probation or correctional custody (Gray, 1996). This dispositional pattern is consistent with what Gray referred to, as the disciplinary welfare philosophy of Hong Kong's juvenile justice system, whereby the "best interests" of the juvenile are balanced with the need to discipline and redirect troublesome youth behaviour (1996). In the early 1990s, the rate of cautioning decreased and custodial sentences remained stable (Gray, 1996).

Given Gray's findings of the 1980s and the early 1990s, how has the system fared more recently? By 1996, the arrest rate for those aged 7 to 17 climbed to 1,047 per 100,000 and the caution rate of 410.8 per 100,000 exceeded the level noted by Gray in 1989. From 1997 onward, however, the juvenile arrest rate has steadily decreased from 937.9 per 100,000 in that year to 869.5 per 100,000 in 2002. Despite this decrease, the percentage of those eligible for cautioning remained steady at slightly over one-half (Table 1). The caution rate also dropped during this period, although there were some fluctuations in 2000 and 2001. While the caution rate has decreased since 1996, the percentage of those arrested receiving a caution has slightly increased. Comparatively, however, the proportion of juveniles receiving cautions in 1987 (61%) was far higher than in any year in the 1990s.

Table 1 Juveniles Arrested and Cautioned Under Police Superintendent's Discretion Scheme

Year	Arrest Rate	% Eligible PSDS	Caution Rate	% of Arrested Cautioned	% Eligible Cautioned
1996	1047.0	54.2	410.8	39.2	72.3
1997	937.9	54.5	347.6	37.1	68.0
1998	925.7	52.0	339.1	36.6	70.4
1999	909.8	54.7	338.4	37.2	68.0
2000	968.6	54.5	397.0	41.1	75.2
2001	932.9	53.5	383.0	41.0	76.8
2002	869.5	54.7	356.6	41.0	75.0

(Source: Annual Reports of Fight Crime Committee, 1996–2002)

Note: In 1995, the upper age of eligibility changed from 16 to 17. "Juvenile" defined as 7 to 17 years of age.

Among those eligible juveniles who did not receive cautions, the police frequently cited the severity of the offense as the primary factor preventing their entry into the PSDS. As Table 2 shows, over 60% of the juveniles were cautioned for shop or miscellaneous theft. Ten percent or less of the juveniles were cautioned for serious assaults. This pattern is consistent with Gray's (1991) findings of earlier periods with the vast majority of cautioned juveniles having committed relatively minor offenses.

The PSDS system, although intended to divert troubled youngsters away from the stigmatizing experience of judicial intervention, does in fact, involve them to regularly contact official control agents. As Table 3 shows, until recently, over 70% of juveniles cautioned under the

Table 2 Offences of Juveniles cautioned under the PSDS

Offence	Year					
	1997	1998	1999	2000	2001	2002
Shop Theft	52.6	55.9	48.9	45.0	46.0	53.4
Misc. Thefts	18.5	18.2	19.8	22.3	23.1	17.3
Wounding & Serious Assault	9.6	8.4	9.5	10.0	9.6	10.0
Robbery	1.1	1.6	1.9	3.3	3.6	2.8
Other	18.1	15.9	19.9	19.5	17.7	12.3
Total (in number)	3,265	3,190	3,216	3,760	3,585	3,345

(Source: Annual Reports of Fight Crime Committee, 1996–2002)

Table 3 Referrals for Juveniles Cautioned Under the PSDS

Referral Organization	Year					
	1997	1998	1999	2000	2001	2002
Juvenile Protection Section (JPS)	85.8	74.6	77.0	73.9	73.2	54.6
Community Support Service Scheme	11.3	24.1	20.6	22.5	21.6	43.2
Social Welfare Department	2.7	1.0	2.2	3.2	5.1	1.5
Education Department	0.2	0.3	0.2	0.4	0.1	0.7
Total (in number)	2,258	2,761	2,724	3,702	3,500	3,952

(Source: Annual Reports of Fight Crime Committee, 1996–2002)
Note: Offenders may have more than one referral; and not all offenders cautioned were referred.

Scheme were referred to the Juvenile Protection Section (JPS) in which the cautioned young person is routinely visited by police officers of this unit. After a JPS officer initially interviews the juvenile and his or her parents at their home, the officer conducts monthly visits to the family to check on the young person's progress in relation to school performance and conduct, leisure time activities and conduct, and family relationships. These visits may be more frequent if the juvenile is considered to be at high risk of engaging in troublesome or delinquent behaviours. The JPS officers visit the homes of about 70 juveniles per month, averaging about four visits per workday with the visits centering on attitudinal and behavioural conformity (e.g. disciplinary welfare concerns) (Chong, 2000). Moreover, the police routinely liaise with social workers and teachers regarding the young persons' behaviour. Although JPS officers are operating in the capacity of social control agents, they recognize that their role is largely as a counsellor to encourage the young persons to abide by the law and to develop healthy relationships with family and friends (Chong, 2000). Compared to social workers, the JPS officer's dual role as control agent and counsellor has a greater deterrent effect such that the juveniles would be less likely to manipulate the police (Chong, 2000).

Once a juvenile is cautioned, he or she may also be referred to, either simultaneously or in lieu of the JPS, other support services offered by the Social Welfare and Education Departments. There are then, a number of branches for controlling and instilling discipline through diversion in Hong Kong. The Community Support Service Scheme (CSSS) has been increasingly used with a disciplinary welfare orientation. According to the Fight Crime Committee (2002), the CSSS, operated by non-governmental organizations (NGOs) is to "encourage juveniles who have infringed the law to return to a decent law abiding life-style", through counselling, job training, skills enhancement, recreation, volunteer work and parent programmes (P.121). Notably, with the formal endorsement of the CSSS in the mid 1997s, the proportion of juveniles referred to JPS steadily declined from 86% in 1997 to 55% by 2002. At the same time, the proportion of juveniles referred to the CSSS grew from 11% in 1997 to 43% by 2002. An evaluation report indicated that the CSSS services have been effective in assisting juveniles (Lo et al., 2003). However, it should be noted here that while the cautioning rate has slightly declined over the 1990s, the nature and extent of control and regulation for diverted youngsters appears to have strengthened with the introduction of the CSSS. Since its formal inception in the mid-1997, the number of referrals has risen from 2,258 in 1997 to nearly 4,000 by 2002. It is also possible that a juvenile may be subjected to a number of services during his or her diversionary period.

As part of the PSDS, the police monitor cautioned juveniles for two years or up until their eighteenth birthday. As Table 4 indicates, less than 20% of cautioned juveniles are rearrested. Age breakdowns indicate that the recidivism rate is highest amongst 12 to 13 year olds (at about 20% in 2000), slightly lower among 14 to 17 year olds (at about 18% in 2000), and followed by 10 to 11 year olds (10%). These rates are not surprising given that the offences for which the juveniles were cautioned were relatively minor and the PSDS emphasis on regular monitoring and regulation of their behaviour. In a later section, we will examine the experiences of a group of cautioned youngsters who participated in an early intervention programme.

As the above discussion indicates, approximately 40% of juvenile arrests resulted in cautions during the latter part of the 1990s, even with the overall decrease in the arrest and caution rates. Important to any discussion of diversion as part of a juvenile justice strategy must

Table 4 Recidivism Rate for Juveniles Cautioned Under the PSDS

Year	Recidivism Rate
1996	15.9%
1997	17.0%
1998	16.5%
1999	13.8%
2000	18.0%

(Source: Annual Reports of the Fight Crime Committee, 1996–2002.)

be the question of what happens to the 60% of arrested juveniles who are not diverted but were sent through the juvenile courts? Based on sentencing data, Gray (1997) found that during the 1980s and into the early 1990s, the juvenile courts took a relatively conservative approach in dealing with young people, using probation orders, often with a residential stay in a probation home, or correctional custody. During the latter part of the 1990s, the rate of probation orders declined. For 1994/95, the rate of probation orders was 138.7 per 100,000 for 15 year olds and under and 341.7 per 100,000 for those between the ages of 16 and 20. By 2002/2003, the rate dropped to 91.0 per 100,000 for youngsters 15 years of age and under, and 258.8 for older adolescents (Census and Statistics Department, 2003). Importantly, however, as Gray (1997) had noted in earlier periods, the majority of young persons placed on probation have not committed serious crimes. This pattern continues to hold true in the latter 1990s, albeit at a slightly lower proportion. For 1995/1996, 82% of young probationers and 78% of older adolescent probationers were convicted of either a property or minor crime. In 2002/ 2003, 67% of young probationers and 58% of older adolescent probationers were convicted of these two categories of crime (Census and Statistics Department, 2003).

The use of correctional custody has a slightly different pattern during this period. As Table 5 shows, the overall custody rate for males has significantly dropped from 727.8 per 100,000 in 1994 to 395.0 per 100,000 in 2002. Consistent over the nine-year period, over 50% of male admissions were for crimes against property or local laws. These decreases are most evident in prison, training centre and drug addiction treatment centre (DATC) admissions. The male admission rates to detention centres declined and then rose in 2000. Among males admitted to prisons in 2001, over 80% of them had no prior institutional sentence. More significantly, 41% of males admitted to the training centres and 50% of those admitted to the detention centres had no prior convictions (Correctional Services Department, 2001).

Table 5   Admission Rates to Correctional Services by Sex and Type of Custody

Year	1994	1995	1996	1997	1998	1999	2000	2001	2002
Males under 21 yrs.									
Prisons	292.8	283.5	230.1	191.5	195.9	203.9	153.0	136.2	140.4
Training Centres	144.9	132.3	91.7	64.1	66.8	70.9	71.9	64.6	55.5
Detention Centre	97.9	93.6	76.6	61.9	53.1	62.7	91.3	103.5	118.9
DATC*	192.2	193.4	180.0	125.3	86.4	59.0	42.1	59.9	57.1
Rehabilitation Centre**	–	–	–	–	–	–	–	–	23.0
Total	727.8	702.9	578.4	442.8	402.2	396.5	358.3	364.3	395.0
Females under 21 yrs.									
Prisons	154.9	218.5	178.6	174.5	108.9	109.9	196.9	444.2	716.5
Training Centres	15.7	12.6	7.8	12.3	4.1	9.8	5.8	5.3	6.3
DATC*	35.0	40.5	38.9	20.9	15.5	12.4	13.6	13.8	8.0
Total	205.6	271.5	225.4	210.6	128.5	132.1	212.1	463.3	730.0

(Source: Census and Statistics Annual Report, 2001–2003)

Note: *   Drug Addiction Treatment Centres

    ** Rehabilitation Centre for males only, operation since 2002

The opposite trend is seen for female admissions. The overall admission rates to custody increased from 205.6 per 100,000 in 1994 to 730.0 per 100,000 by 2002, although it is noted that there were significant drops in 1998 and 1999. Most of this increase has been for admissions to prison. In 1994, 58% of female admissions were for local law violations, but by 2002, this offence type accounted for over 80% of all young female admissions. Over 95% of females under 21 years of age admitted to prisons in 2001 had no prior institutional sentence. Among females admitted to the training centre, no one of them had a prior conviction in 2000 and 2001 (Correctional Services Department, 2001). Although a discussion of this current trend in female custody is beyond the scope of this article, it is important to note that it is related to the conviction of young women from Mainland China who have been convicted of breaching the conditions of their immigration visas such as overstaying and working without a permit.

From the discussion above, there has been a decline in the rate of young persons entering into many key points within the juvenile justice system by the end of the 1990s and the early part of the new millennium, from arrests to cautioning to probation and custody (with the exception of female prison admissions). Despite these decreases, many of the trends in the 1980s, identified by Gray (1996), continue to permeate the system, in particular, the inclusion of juveniles arrested on relatively minor offenses into diversion as well as juveniles with limited or no prior convictions being sent to custody, largely for property and local law violations. One significant change since the 1980s is the increase in the support services for diverted youngsters, most notably through the CSSS. Since its inception in mid-1997, an increasing number of diverted youngsters have been referred to CSSS. In effect, the CSSS has served as another branch within diversion for facilitating the regulation and control of young persons. In the following section, I provide a description and evaluation of a diversion programme in Hong Kong, originated in the latter part of 1997 and continues to the present.

Project X: A Diversion Programme

Tuen Mun, a large residential district, has been clearly recognized as an area in Hong Kong that has faced a number of community stressors and social problems, especially with delinquency, triad activities and drug use among its teenagers. In Tuen Mun, juveniles account for a large proportion of all reported crime committed. In the late 1990s, for example, they represented nearly 20 percent of all arrests in this community, largely on offences related to theft, shoplifting and assault (Tuen Mun Fight Crime Committee, 1999). The Tuen Mun community, particularly the police, has taken an active role in trying to address these problems. The police in this district operate eight early intervention programmes, six of which are based on a multi-agency approach and operate collaboratively with the Social Welfare Department, Education Department, and a local university.

Project X has been deemed to be one of the most popular programmes among the eight intervention programmes (Tuen Mun Project Group, 1998). Project X adopts a multi-disciplinary approach, and is based on a mentoring scheme in which juvenile offenders and other high risk youth referred by the Police, Social Welfare Department or the Hong Kong Federation of Youth Group are paired up with a university student for after care supervision. In this way, the university students are "assistants" to the social workers and police in relatively minor cases. The mentor is given training on leadership skills, law and order, crime and drug use trends and information on support agencies. Upon entering the programme, the youth and the mentor are supposed to maintain regular contact, and the mentor is given a pager in case of emergencies. During this contact, the mentors' main duties are to engage their mentees in conventional social activities and inculcate them with positive social, emotional and ethical concepts. The ultimate aims are to prevent the youth from engaging in high risk behaviours and crime through mentoring/role modelling, and a support system, and to provide university students practical training and experience in working with youth in the community (Tuen Mun Fight Crime Committee, 1999). The following section describes the referral process during the first three years of the project and the experiences of the clients and mentors for one cohort of clients.

Referrals and Counselling Procedure

As Table 6 shows, Project X referrals come largely from the Police Juvenile Protection Service unit, but also from Tuen Mun non-government groups and the primary and secondary schools in the area. During the first three years of the project, over one-half of the referrals were from the police. Cases are assessed by a referral panel (i.e. JPS officer, police community relations officer and a social worker) to see whether the youngsters are suitable for the programme. If the case is not accepted due to the special circumstances of the case or the client is not suitable, it is referred back to the originating source.

Table 6 Referral Agency and Number of Clients Between 1997–1999

Referral Agency	Percentage of Clients
Police — JPS	55.5
HK Fed. of Youth Groups	11.0
Other Community NGOs	2.7
Schools	30.6
Total (in number)	146

(Source: Police Community Relations Office, Tuen Mun)

The panel understands that the mentors are volunteers who have no previous experience in dealing with problematic young people. In order to guarantee the personal safety of the mentors, only those kids who are considered to be "easy-to-handle" or "low-risk" will be nominated. As Table 7 indicates, the majority of cases referred by the Hong Kong Police involve youngsters who have been arrested for some form of minor theft. Only a few males committed relatively serious crimes like arson, assault and burglary. About one-fourth of the females referred to Project X were arrested on an assault offence.

Table 7 Breakdown of Referral Clients: Arrests by Type of Offence (1997–1999)

Offence	% Male	% Female	% All Clients
Shop Theft	35.3	56.7	43.2
Miscellaneous Theft	31.4	13.3	24.7
Unlawful Assembly	3.9	–	2.5
Arson	2.0	–	1.2
Common Assault	2.0	3.3	2.5
Dangerous Drugs	2.0	–	1.2
Equipped for Stealing	5.8	–	3.7
Burglary	3.9	–	2.5
Indecent Assault	2.0	–	1.2
Tampering with Vehicle	3.9	–	2.5
Assault Occasioning Actual Bodily Harm	3.9	26.7	12.3
Criminal Damage	3.9	–	2.5
Total (in number)	51	30	81

(Source: Police Community Relations Office, Tuen Mun)

If the case is considered to be suitable, it will then pass to the mentor. Each mentor is assigned two youngsters. After detailed information of the client has been passed to the mentor, the mentor has to arrange a home visit and contact the client as soon as possible so as to understand the actual situation of the client and his or her family. The scope of problems that the mentor has to handle includes the client's personal, emotional, academic and family problems. Moreover, the mentor also needs to give advice to the client's parents on supervision and communication with their child. A bi-monthly report has to be submitted to the Project X Committee. The mentors also need to attend seminars once every two months in which they can share their experiences with other mentors and social workers. If the mentor finds that the clients are not suitable for the project after serving him or her for a period of time, the mentor has to write a report to the Committee and state the reasons for why the mentee is unsuitable. If the reasons are accepted, the case will be referred back to the originating source.

Programme Impact

From 1999 to 2001, we examined the programme's impact on the participants' attitudes and behaviours and the nature of the contact and relationship between the mentors and the participants (Joe Laidler and Loh, 2002). Our evaluation design was based on a longitudinal study of the impact of juvenile justice intervention programmes overseas (Austin et al., 1990) and involved surveying participants at two time points — at the time of placement and twelve to eighteen months later.

At the Time of Placement (Time 1)

During the study period, 58 youths were eligible to participate in Project X. However, 11 of them refused to be surveyed, nine could not be located, and one dropped out of the programme. Of the 37 participants interviewed at the time of placement, the majority was male (27 or 73%). All but two of them were born in Hong Kong. The male participants were slightly younger than the females with an average age of 12.6 and females were 14.2 years. The majority of participants lived with both parents (32 or 86%). All of them were still attending school. Seventy percent of the males were in Form One or lower (Primary 6 and below). Given the slightly older age of the females, they were enrolled in Form One to Form 5. The average academic result of females was 47.5 compared to that of the males at 50.

The average number of people living with them was four (males and females). The majority of their fathers worked full-time (32 or 86%) in a variety of "blue collar" occupations including taxi and truck drivers, security guards, construction workers, and air conditioner repairmen. The majority of their mothers stayed at home to take care of the family, but 40% (or 15) of their mothers also worked either full- or part-time in blue collar occupations including waitress, shop assistant, security guard, hawker, domestic worker, and clerical worker. The respondents received on average HK$139 for males and HK$160 for females in pocket money each week. Eight of the ten female participants had committed a shoplifting offence. Fifteen of the 27 male participants had committed an offence, principally shoplifting also. Of the remaining boys, they reported committing minor offenses, including stealing bicycles, throwing objects from a height, loitering, robbery, fighting and running away from home.

Aside from the demographic information, we also asked them about their involvement and views about school life. Males had mixed feelings about liking school and spent little time on the weekends for studying. Over 60% of them studied on weekday evenings. Boys generally had positive attitudes towards their teachers and their lessons. Females had mixed feelings about their schools, and did not spend a great deal of time on the weekends for studying. However, the majority of females spent most of their weekday afternoons and evenings for studying. The girls also generally had positive attitudes towards schools, their teachers and their lessons.

Male and female participants tended to spend weekday afternoons and evenings in some form of interaction with their family members (talking and playing). On the weekends, however, 37% of males and only 10% of females reported spending quite a bit or a great deal of time with their families. The majority of boys and girls reported feeling close to their families and believed they could talk with their family members. However, 43% of the boys and 20% of the girls felt pressure from their families to do well in school.

Nearly all of them report having a particular group of friends whom they enjoyed spending time with. One half of the girls and 21% of the boys reported spending quite a bit or a great deal of time on the weekends with their peers. Boys tended to play with their friends on weekday evenings more often than the girls. This is very likely due to greater parental restrictions on girls during the evening hours. According to the participants, the majority of their friends did not engage in troublesome or delinquent activities.

Participants were also asked about their beliefs. Over half of the male and female participants indicated that making a good impression is more important than telling the truth to parents and teachers. Approximately 40% believed that making a good impression is more important than telling the truth to their friends. One third of males believed that it was okay to lie to keep friends out of trouble. Forty-four percent of them also believed its acceptable to beat someone up if they started it first. By comparison, 60% of the females believed that it is alright to lie if it keeps your friends out of trouble and to beat up another person if they started the fight. Despite these beliefs, the majority of them believed that young people should care for their parents' health. Importantly, while 80% of the girls turned to their friends for help and advice, 41% of the boys turned to their parents for advice.

For the participants, leisure activities were principally concentrated around studying, shopping, going to arcades, hanging around in public places, sports (males more than females), playing computers, watching television, talking on the phone and reading various books, magazines and comics.

The participants were asked to indicate the frequency of their involvement in risky and delinquent behaviours. Less than one-third of the boys reported smoking or drinking alcohol. Over 50% had gambled during the past year. Two-thirds of them also reported hanging out in public areas or arcades, with the majority doing so at least once a week, if not more often. Slightly under 50% of them had bullied others during the past year with many reporting doing so at least once a week. Forty-eight percent of the boys reported getting into a fight during the past year.

Overall, the majority of females were not engaging in risky or delinquent behaviours. However, 70% of them indicated that they smoked on occasion, 50% had drunk alcohol in the last year. Eighty percent of them regularly hung out in public places. Sixty percent of them also reported bullying others with the majority of them doing it at least once a week, if not more. Forty percent of them reported associating with Triads at least once a week.

Overall, the participants had positive attitudes to school, teachers and their parents, were relatively close to their families and friends, were involved in conventional leisure activities and were generally not engaging in delinquent behaviours (with the exception of smoking, drinking, and bullying).

Participants One Year On (Time 2)

Interviews after 12/18 months revealed that in terms of family relationships, the participants had comparably better levels of interaction with family members than reported earlier. Peer relationships and involvement remained relatively constant over the study period, although fewer girls reported spending quite a lot or a great deal of their time on the weekends with friends.

There was little change in their beliefs at this later period. However, a great proportion of girls had turned to their parents for help and advice (43% at Time 2 compared to 20% at Time 1). Participants reported similar patterns of time spent on leisure activities at Time 2 compared to Time 1. The participants reported being slightly less involved in risky and delinquent behaviours. There were relatively few changes in self-reported delinquency among males. At Time 2, fewer females reported smoking, drinking alcohol and bullying others during the past year. Nearly 30% reported not hanging out in public places.

Participants were also asked at this later time about their experiences and relationships with the mentors and Project X. Of the 29 interviewed at Time 2, 17 of them provided details of their experiences. Seven participants indicated that they had established good relationships with their mentors. Some of them reported talking mostly on the phone about life, others reported going out with the mentors to watch movies, or going out for snacks. The male participants enjoyed having female mentors as this gave them an opportunity to talk to someone of the opposite sex and to ask for advice about personal relationships. One male participant was very enthusiastic about his relationship, and noted how this developed over time as follows.

At first, I didn't understand the Project. They only organized one tea gathering. There was no other function. All my friends who joined Project X had the same impression. After the first meeting, all the mentors, and the Project as well, seemed to disappear. I didn't think that they gave us any assistance. Although my mentor didn't call me, I called my mentor actively. Now we have established a very good relationship. We call each other every day, we talk about minor things. Sometimes, he gives me advice. Even though I don't listen to him, we still communicate very well.

The other ten participants felt indifferent towards their relationship with their mentors, believing that they had not established much of a bond with the mentors. This was sometimes due to lack of contact but often it was related to their inability to communicate with the mentors.

Mentors' Experiences

The study also collected information from the mentors to examine the extent and nature of the contact with the youth. During the study period, 25 of the 29 Project X mentors turned in a total of 276 monthly contact sheets on 48 participants. Based on their reports, a total of 536 calls were made during the study period, with an average of 2 phone calls per month. Each phone call lasted, on average, 9 minutes. Mentors reported spending an average of 11 minutes making phone calls to the participants each month. Aside from setting up times to meet, the nature of the calls covered a range of areas including talking about school, homework, studying, examinations and results, private tutorials, love affairs, friends, parents and holidays. Interestingly, there was no contact made via the internet (ICQ or email).

Face to face interaction occurred less frequently than telephone contact. Of the 48 participants, eight of them never met with their mentors during the entire study period except for the first introduction session. The frequency of face-to-face contact between the mentors and the participants varied from once to eleven times. The total number of face to face contact was 97. Only one or two of the face to face meetings were organized by the Project with visits to Ocean Park and barbecues. On average, mentors made 0.35 face to face contacts per month. These face to face contacts lasted, on average, three hours (range from 15 minutes to 11.25 hours). Some mentors organized their own get-togethers with the participants and involved celebrating birthdays, shopping, watching a movie, having a meal or snack, playing sports, visiting the university and visiting a museum, etc.

Based on mentors' feedback, they often experienced problems in trying to engage the participants, and found it difficult to develop rapport with the mentees. Mentors described their frustration and communication problems:

- Our conversations on the phone are like "dead air".
- We have nothing to talk about.
- The client didn't want to walk with me and walked very slowly.
- The client is too passive and quiet.
- He is not willing to meet me.
- The client didn't like me because I am older than him.
- I don't know how to deal with him.
- He only says, "I don't know".
- He is not willing to talk and has no opinions to my suggestions.
- It's difficult to find topics and interests in common.
- The client thinks it's boring to go out with me.
- The juvenile is very young. It is quite difficult to communicate with him.

Although the mentors and mentees were relatively close in age, developmentally and practically, they were at different life stages. This may account for the infrequency of face-to-face contact. Some mentors took the initiative to resolve these communication obstacles by contacting mentees' parents or writing letters to mentees to facilitate interaction. There were several cases in which the mentors described positive and fulfilling relationships developed with their mentees. In these cases, mentors took an active role in learning about the interests of the mentees, and initiated activities enjoyed by the mentees.

From this study, it appears that Project X, as a type of police diversion programme, targets youngsters who have committed very minor offenses. The survey data showed that most of the youngsters, who although sometimes got themselves into risky situations or engaged in troublesome behaviours, generally had positive attitudes towards their families and schools. These attitudes and behaviours did not change significantly over the study period. Official and self-report data indicate that the Project X participants did not progress into more risky or delinquent behaviours. Only two participants were arrested during the study period, while some of the Project X participants and mentors found the mentoring programme rewarding. The basic foundation of mentoring programmes is relationship building between the young person and the mentor. Although one would presume that this relationship can develop quickly, especially when the young person and the mentor are from the same generation, this relationship needs time and support to develop. Mentors and participants have independently suggested that they are not from the same generation. As noted above, the majority of mentors and the participants indicated that they were not able to "talk" and "communicate" with each other, and were usually at a loss for knowing what to say.

Conclusion

It is difficult to predict whether the youngsters participating in Project X — a kind of police diversion programme — would have engaged in more serious crime if they had not been cautioned or referred to the Project. Some of the Project X participants would have also been subjected to monthly visits by their JPS officer, and hence, their attitudes and behaviours would be under greater scrutiny and regulation. Project X's effects would be impossible to disentangle from those of the JPS supervision. Moreover, although Project X mentors are tasked with helping to shape and redirect the troubled youth towards conventional attitudes and behaviours, the above discussion suggests that this is exceedingly difficult to accomplish. It may well be that these youngsters, who committed minor offences but had positive attitudes and involvement with their families and schools, are gradually and naturally maturing.

It was in the 1980s that Gray (1996) observed the rise of the disciplinary welfare orientation in Hong Kong's juvenile justice system. From the 1990s to present, this philosophy toward treating the problems of young people in Hong Kong prevails despite declining rates throughout the system. In terms of diversion, the CSSS has introduced another branch or layer for trying to redirect and instill discipline and conventional attitudes on youngsters who find themselves in sometimes risky situations. Project X illustrates the continued emphasis on disciplinary welfare within police diversion as well as Hong Kong's juvenile justice system more generally. Given that the vast majority of cautioned youngsters have no prior legal history and have committed minor offences, are such attempts to control, regulate and redirect these types of young people to conventionality really necessary?

7

Community Support Service Scheme — Project Phoenix

Koon-mei Lee

The issue of youth-at-risk (YAR) has raised much concern from the public and the government. There is an outcry for more allocation of resources for services to the YAR, and more funding should be pooled into related services. The recent expansion of Community Support Service Schemes (CSSSs), District Outreaching Service, Young Night Drifters Service etc are some typical examples (SWD, 2002b).

Project Phoenix — Community Support Service Scheme (PP-CSSS) is one of the existing service projects for YAR. The term "youth-at-risk" has taken on some broad connotations but in the current context, it refers to those juveniles aged from 10 to below 18 who have committed trivial offences and have been put under the Police Superintendents' Discretion Scheme (PSDS), that is the clientele of PP. Any youngster has the chance to fall into this category. They may just be normal youth who happen to act against the law in a certain context. Despite the trivial nature of many juvenile offences, it should not be overlooked as it is upsetting both to society and the victims. With the existence of the YAR, society is at-risk too. On the contrary, young people are risking their future if they cannot be made aware of the negative consequences of their offences. PP is based on the philosophy of helping the youth clarify values and exert some control over themselves, to help them make choices about their own lives and future. Besides, it also serves to fill the service gap that no other youth service has ever targeted before.

A review report in 1997 (Lo et al.) has confirmed the effectiveness and supported the establishment of CSSSs in helping young offenders, a kind of YAR. The findings of the study are valuable references for service providers and policy makers to know how far the projects work and what aspects of the projects have to be improved. The establishment of PP is not to promote "net widening", instead it provides voluntary-based follow-up service for the cautioned juvenile offenders and their parents. Youngsters are being referred to PP due to a clear-cut reason — law breaking. Their needs as revealed from the law breaking behaviours are multi-faceted. This paper aims to introduce the Project, including its historical development, service objectives, guiding concepts and service contents. A current study exploring the effectiveness of PP will also be introduced. How the services of the Project could be improved will be discussed at the end of the paper.

Historical Development of Project Phoenix

Project Phoenix — Community Support Service Scheme originated from the Project Phoenix Counselling Service which started on 1st January 1992. "Phoenix" is a lifelong bird in legend. It means "life beyond death". We believe that the juveniles who have committed crimes have potential and opportunities to turn over a new leaf and be law-abiding citizens.

Initially, the Project was a self-financed one-man project which was initiated by the Methodist Centre in Hong Kong. The Wan Chai Police Station was invited to co-operate in the Project, and police officers helped solicit written consent from parents of the youth who were under PSDS. The social worker from the Centre collected the consent forms from the Police Station and then offered follow-up services for the juveniles and their parents. (Lo and Kam, 1994).

The idea behind the Project caught the attention and recognition of the government. In October 1994, the Social Welfare Department (SWD) started to subvent the Project as a two-year pilot-project (Lo, 1998; Lo et al., 2001). Since then, it has been renamed as Project Phoenix — Community Support Service Scheme (PP-CSSS). The government financed the Project with the objective to provide community rehabilitation service to the YAR. With five workers in the Project, the target group of the Project are children and young people at-risk and are residing, working, studying or cautioned by the police under the PSDS in Hong Kong Island. In this aspect, the target group encompasses different kinds of YAR, whether law-abiding or not. But the Project is aimed at the cautioned youth as the core target. As manpower, resources and service boundary expanded, the social workers of PP started to make liaison with all police stations on Hong Kong Island. Also, more police officers shared the value of a multi-disciplinary work mode. They helped improve the referral procedure by informing the Project in advance, so that the social workers in the Project could directly contact the cautioned juveniles and their parents at the police stations on the days of caution. The number of referrals has risen largely from 39 per year in 1992 to 448 per year in 2002.

In 1994 the SWD also ran two units of CSSSs at Kowloon East and Kowloon West for young probationers and subvented the Hong Kong Federation of Youth Groups to run another unit of CSSS at New Territories West. All the units of CSSSs were the review research targets of Lo et al. (1997). The research confirmed the effectiveness of CSSSs and recommended the setting up of more CSSSs to help the YAR so that cautioned juveniles under PSDS in the whole territory can be served. After the review, the CSSSs became a long-term subvented service of the government and opinions were more inclined towards having more establishments of CSSSs, thus all Hong Kong PSDS juveniles can be served.

In April 2000, the Project Phoenix signed the Funding and Services Agreement (FSA) with the SWD, confining its target clientele to the cautioned juveniles who live in Hong Kong Island and outlying Islands. Besides, the Project has to fulfill the output standards of 210 cases/year, while 145 closed cases should have achieved its working goals. The Project also needs to have 3,480 direct contact hours with cases each year. In April 2001, the FSA was revised, two outcome indicators (i.e. more than 90% of the service target should have no recidivism during the supervision period and more than 85% of the service target should remain either in study or work at the time of case closing) have been added. The adding of these requirements indicates that the government (funding body) and society request outcome effectiveness and accountability of the Project.

In October 2001, three more units of CSSSs run by Non-governmental Organizations (NGOs), which cover Kowloon East, Kowloon West, and New Territories East, were set up. They were all attached with their Agencies' Integrated Children and Youth Services Centres (ICYSCs). PP was also requested to attach to an agency's ICYSC in October 2002. Consequently, there are now five units of CSSSs from NGOs which are affiliated with ICYSCs.

Service Objectives of Project Phoenix

At the beginning, PP had 4 main service objectives (Lo and Kam, 1994). They were:

1. To help targeted youth to clarify their values;
2. To help them learn socially acceptable behaviours and values;
3. To improve their relationship with other systems, e.g. family, school and peers; and
4. To develop their leadership skills and encourage them to serve the community.

When the government began to subvent the Project in 1994, an information paper on CSSS (SWD, 1994) that stated out the government's expectations on the objectives of the Project was issued. The FSA (SWD, 2000) and Information Paper on Referral Mechanisms for CSSS (SWD, 2002a) further concretized CSSS's purposes and objectives. They confirmed the purpose of CSSS is to assist the targeted young people to re-integrate into the community, eliminate their deviant and unlawful behaviours, and reduce their likelihood of law infringement. The objectives of PP in working with the targeted young people are re-stated as (Methodist Centre, 2000):

1. To reintegrate the targeted children and young people into the education system or initiate their entrance into the work force;
2. To help them develop socially acceptable behaviours;
3. To redirect their energies into constructive and legitimate channels;
4. To enhance their development through strengthening the community support network; and
5. To lead them to become law abiding citizens.

Guiding Concepts of Project Phoenix

For decades, numerous overseas and local studies have been carried out to explore the causes of juvenile delinquency (Ng et al., 1975; Cheung and Ng, 1988; Cheung, 1993; Wong et al., 1995; Krohn et al., 1996; Lee, 1996; Weis et al., 1996; Jang and Smith, 1997; Lam, 1998; Wong, 1997 &1999). However, no single theory is adequate in providing a comprehensive explanation of delinquency. The explanatory power increases when more major theories are integrated (Elliott, et al., 1985; Thornberry, 1987; Wong, 1999).

The guiding concepts that the Project employ are those of the Social

Bond Theory of Hirschi (1969). Hirschi stated if people are tightly attached to the basic values and expected behaviors of society, they are behaviorally restricted and therefore unlikely to commit delinquent or criminal behaviours (Hirschi, 1969; Thornberry et. al., 1991; Bynum and Thompson, 1992; Trojanowicz and Morash, 1992). In his theory, four elements of bond: **belief, commitment, involvement** and **attachment**, are emphasized. The model assumes that weakened bond will result in the commitment of delinquency. But such behaviours need to be learned and reinforced before being enacted. It is believed that attachment to delinquent peers is directly related to delinquency (Thornberry et al., 1991; Trojanowicz and Morash, 1992). This conceptual framework guides the practice of PP.

PP focuses on strengthening the youth's **belief** in the moral validity of rules, activating their **commitment** to social values and norms, revitalizing their **involvement** in conventional activities, encouraging their **attachment** to conventional others but discouraging their **attachment** with delinquent peers. The working themes are developed from the said objectives. The conceptual framework that guides the operation of the Project is presented in Figure 1.

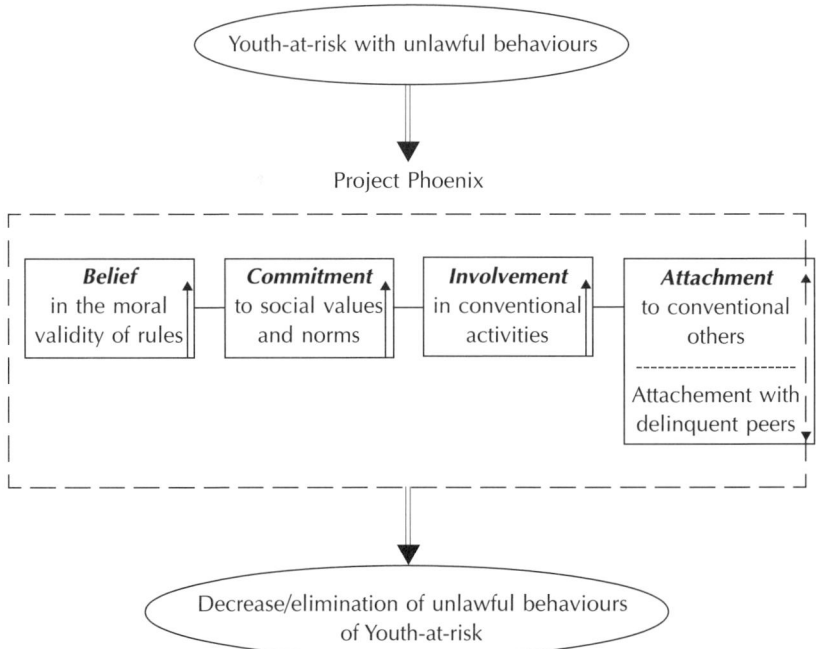

Figure 1 Conceptual Framework of Project Phoenix

Service Contents

The intervention direction of PP is multi-systemic (Lo et. al., 2001) and it deals with many aspects of youngsters' lives. Diversified Case Management Model (DCMM) is employed by the Project in its operation (Lo, 1998; Lo et al., 2001). It jointly employs casework and group work approaches in its service provision. Case-in-group services that supplement with community networking activities are delivered. Every newly referred PSDS youngster is taken care of by a caseworker and he or she is encouraged to join the orientation group of the Project. The DCMM is presented in the following diagram (Figure 2):

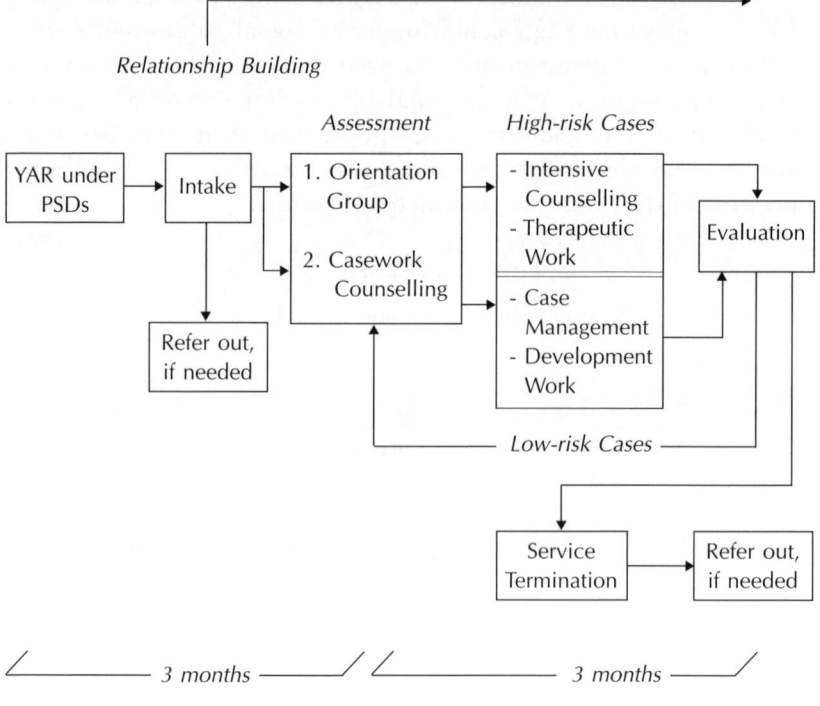

Figure 2 Diversified Case Management Model

In the intake process, workers of PP will first assess the youth's suitability in joining the orientation group. The willingness of the youngsters and their parents will be taken into consideration. Some of the youngsters are hesitant in joining the groups because they are afraid of meeting strangers. They may feel uncomfortable and uneasy at the beginning. The workers will try to alleviate their distress by ensuring them that more friends will be made after joining the groups, and will encourage them to look at it as a challenge. Some parents have doubts in letting their children join the groups or activities because they fear other participants will have undesirable influences on their kids. The workers will acknowledge their concern and maintain continuous contact and communication with them in order to gain their trust. If they trust the workers and understand the purpose of the Project, their worries will be greatly minimized. Even if some of them do not join the groups or activities of the Project, individual, family or group counselling will still be offered.

A group is a social microcosm of society (Yalom, 1985). The youngsters have to interact and learn to cooperate with others in the groups. Through group work, workers can have better knowledge of the youth. It also helps speed up the process of assessment, and provides more materials for the workers in individual counselling. On the basis of information gained in individual counselling and/or group work sessions, assessment of the cases can be made. If young people realize the importance of law and order, their re-offending is unlikely. Intensive individual counselling and therapeutic work are provided to high risk cases, while developmental work and continuous case management service are available to relatively low-risk cases. The youth are helped in defining their need or difficulties more clearly and are made aware of the cost of committing crimes, while their choices for alternative behavioural patterns are expanded (John, 1999). Individual counselling plus group work assist the YAR to overcome their difficulties in personal and social development, in particular their offending behaviours. Their social skills, interpersonal relationships and life aspirations are enhanced. Their undesirable attitudes and behaviours are also positively modified.

The engagement of young people in conventional activities, such as school and work, can preoccupy them so they do not become involved in delinquent behaviours. Educational and/or vocational guidance are offered to the youth in the Project. They and their parents regard workers in the Project as resource persons who can provide them with relevant information and assistance.

The strengths of youth, rather than their deficiencies, are built on. Volunteer services, community service activities, adventurous programmes, inter-flow learning trips and positive reinforcement schemes are organized regularly, so opportunities are provided to build up their successful experience, and develop their positive self-image and sense of social responsibility. The Project organizes programmes jointly with other community organizations. For example, since 1998, anti-crime campaigns have been launched yearly between the Project and the Wan Chai Fight Crime Committee. In the campaigns, the youth acts as "fight crime angels". They help advocate the importance of abiding law and order, and educate citizens on how to prevent crimes. The youth are empowered through community participation and social recognition.

It is believed that youth, who attach to conventional others, such as parents, desirable peers, teachers, and social workers, are sensitive to positive wishes and values, and are, unlikely to engage in delinquent acts. Various relevant workshops and seminars for parents, teachers, and social workers, related to the target youth group, have been organized. Relevant systems are worked with so as to strengthen the support network for young people. Parents are invited to participate in the intervention process and serve as supporting resources for the young people. Usually, when young people are invited to attend interviews or group sessions with the workers, they often arrive with a friend or some friends. If their friends take part in the interviews or group sessions, it will provide an opportunity for the workers to engage the YAR more effectively. It is acknowledged that peer influence sometimes is greater than family influence.

It is believed that a multi-disciplinary rapport is crucial for the service provision of PP. The workers of PP work closely with Juvenile Protection Section of the Police and officers of different police stations. Sharing sessions are organized and the cooperation and referral mode are continually reviewed and improved. When terminating the cases, upon their consent the youngsters will be assisted to participate in services of nearby social organizations.

Effectiveness of Project Phoenix

The author conducted quasi-experimental research on Project Phoenix in 2001 (Lee, 2001). A brief summary of the project will be introduced to discuss the impact and effectiveness of working with YAR. Twelve young offenders under PSDS — 6 PP cases and 6 non-cases were interviewed twice (pre-test at July 2000 and post-test at January 2001) through the use of a qualitative research method. They were classified as experimental group (PP cases — E1 to E6) and control group (non-PP cases — C1 to C6).

Respondents in the experimental group have reported stronger positive changes at post-test stage in various aspects. The impact of PP has been encouraging on both minor and persistent young offenders. As articulated by all respondents in the experimental group, *"helping"* is the main rehabilitative function of the Project. They all joined the Project voluntarily and their attendance rate was 100%. Besides positive behavioural changes, the respondents in the experimental group also showed progress in their academic work and enjoyed happier lives. The recidivist rate of the respondents in the experimental group and control group were respectively 17% (1 case) and 67% (4 cases). All respondents in the experimental group maintained their study or work, and were reported to have put greater effort on their study and improved academically.

At pre-test interviews, all respondents except E4 and C2 claimed that they had good relationships with their parents. E4 reported great improvement in her relationship with family members at post-test, while C2 reported an unfavourable relationship with his family members. Favourable attachment to parents is a protective factor but does not guarantee non-delinquent youngsters. E4 in the experimental group was a typical example.

> E4: "I change because of a group of people who concern me. The group includes my family members."

Five respondents in the experimental group (E1, E2, E3, E5 & E6) had strong attachment to their academic work, while only one respondent in the control group (C6) paid more effort on academic work. The risk of youngsters re-committing crimes were greatly reduced when they focused on their study, according to the opinions of respondents in the experimental group. E4 in the experimental group shared that she was happy though it was hard to work. E4 admitted she would not steal anymore because she could legally earn money. She behaved in a law-abiding way because of her strong attachment to work.

Five out of six respondents in the experimental group (E1–E5) decreased or cut their attachment to previous undesirable peers. They became aware of the dangers of associating with them in terms of re-offending. However, half of the respondents in the control group still got along with undesirable peers who might foster their re-offending.

> E1: "I have fewer external friends (undesirable peers) and I haven't kept much contact with them."

> E4: "I don't go along with the previous friends (undesirable peers) anymore (after conviction)."

Life goals and pursuit of future prospects might bond one to conventional values and norms. All respondents in the experimental group shared their life goals and views on the future at post-test interviews. However, the life goals and future aspiration of respondents in the control group remained vague both at pre-test and post-test interviews. The commitment to social values and norms was stronger for those in the experimental group than those in the control group. But one should be reminded that the stronger commitment to social values and norms could not be served as comprehensive buffer against re-offending. E4 in the experimental group was an official recidivist (shop-theft).

Three respondents in the experimental group who had joined the activities of PP reported various positive experiences. The effectiveness of the programme activities has been confirmed.

> E2: "Those activities can train up my physical fitness. I also learn to be cooperative and independent."

> E4: "I want to join those activities for a long time. Now I have the opportunity. Those activities are interesting and meaningful."

> E5: "I have joined the volunteer service and have chances to know more new arrivals. They are not that 'bad'."

All respondents in the experimental group received individual counselling service. This was most helpful and meaningful to them as each session could be tailored to each individual's needs.

The deviant values of young respondents contributed to their commitment of offences. If they could gain positive insight and learn proper values out of their arrests, they are likely to become more law-abiding. At post-test, three respondents in the experimental group (E1, E3 & E6) had positive changes in their behaviours, while four respondents in the control group (C1, C2, C3 & C6) were indifferent, and all had a record of recidivism.

Positive results could be seen once young offenders refocused on their study. Their academic achievement would enhance their self-concept and others' perception of them. They became happier and enjoyed the improvement of academic performance and did not re-offend.

Attachment to undesirable peers is undoubtedly a significant cause of juvenile delinquency. A promising buffer solution was for juvenile delinquents to keep a distance or sever their relationship with undesirable peers. Positive peers support, including inviting young offenders to join in extra-curricular activities, was encouraged so they could constructively establish attachment to another group of desirable peers.

To induce *"hope"* and *"future"* for the YAR is crucial. It is believed if they have proper hopes, they will be more conscious of the cost and benefit of re-offending and will work harder towards a better future.

An initial stage of establishing attachment is needed before young offenders can be modified. Various interventions should be carried out at the same time. These include encouraging them to join activities, and helping them develop attachment to parents and study. The Project would not underestimate its impact on the young offenders because it is also one of the desirable conventional others.

Conclusion

The rehabilitative function of the Project was recognized by the respondents in the experimental group and confirmed in the related research (Lo et al., 1997). The youngsters in the experimental group gained greater positive changes. It suggests that CSSS service should be adopted and expanded.

In the experimental group, respondents reported that the individual casework counselling service was most useful to them. Some commented that these group programmes and activities, such as volunteer service and adventurous training, had enriched their exposure and development. Their experience indicates that individual casework counselling should be the core service mode for young offenders in the Project. While the value of group programmes and activities was confirmed, they are suggested to serve as supplements to counselling service.

Ideas for improving the service include:
1. paying special attention to those YAR who have prior offenses;
2. bearing in mind that good attachment with family could serve as a protective factor against re-offending of young people;
3. embracing the aim of helping young people refocus their effort on study or work;
4. guiding the youth to analyze the impact of peers influence on them;
5. fostering positive peers support by encouraging them to join extra-curricular activities or programmes of the Project; and
6. inspiring them to think on their future goals.

There have been suggestions of developing a risk assessment tool to assist workers so they have better planning on services provision. More attention should be paid to high-risk cases as they need intensive and multi-level treatments.

PP was attached to an ICYSC (Intergrated Children and Youth Service Centre) in October, 2002. The newly formed structure provides flexibility for the management to exercise her autonomy on manpower re-allocation. Due to manpower limitation in the past, the five frontline workers of PP could not open all PSDS cases shortly after referral. A waiting list existed and it affected the capacity to handle the case. Under the structure of the ICYSC, more manpower could be deployed to handle the cases. The wait-list phenomenon has been improved. If the workers in the ICYSC work with both PSDS youngsters and "normal youth", integration of young people as a whole can also be actualized. The youngsters in the Project can have more opportunities to mix with other youth in various programmes. The labeling effect on the YAR in the Project can be minimized.

Besides, focusing on the work with YAR and their parents, we also need to keep an eye on issues which affect our clients. The age of criminal responsibility has been raised to 10 instead of 7 since July 2003. This legal movement will definitely affect our clients and our service indirectly. As responsible service providers, we have the obligation to provide our opinions and comments on the issue. An effective service requires active collaboration of a variety of statutory and voluntary agencies, and have to be monitored and evaluated.

We have to admit that the Project cannot totally stop young people from re-offending and also cannot solve all problems of YAR. We have to collaborate with the society at large to give support to our young people. We are contributing to help them exert control over themselves, and make choices about their own lives.

8

Effectivesness of Services to "Youth-at-Risk":

The Case of Outreaching Social Work

Howard Chi-ho Cheng

There are various kinds of services available to the at-risk youth who exhibit different degrees of risky behaviours. Among the services, Outreaching Social Work (OSW) has the longest history of development since June 1979. In this paper, the first focus will be on discussing the relationship between service effectiveness and service improvement in the case of OSW service as this type of youth service is designed specifically for youth-at-risk (YAR).

An evaluation of the history and advantages of OSW service evaluation in Hong Kong will then be pointed out. There will also be an analysis of why some youth workers in OSW service resist service evaluation. Finally, the discussion will shift towards possible future development of OSW in context of service evaluation and effectiveness based on the quality improvement process model.

Measurability of Human Services

In the Social Welfare Department Annual Report 2001, the Director of Social Welfare wrote in the foreword:

> Year 2001 was a year of major breakthroughs. The long-debated Lump Sum Grant System was formally introduced in January 2001. This new mode of subvention, characterized by flexibility, autonomy and accountability in the use of resources is now practiced by 150 NGOs. Together they account for 96% of the total recurrent welfare subventions. A revised system for allocating new service units based on quality, cost-effectiveness and innovation was put firmly in place during the year (Director of Social Welfare, 2002: 1).

The terms "accountability", "quality", "cost-effectiveness" and "innovation" have been greatly promoted in recent years. All NGO workers, including youth workers, would find these concepts familiar. But at the same time they would also hold a mixed love hate attitude towards these terms. Professional social workers understand they have entered a period of accountability, responsibility and evidence-based practice as social services, including youth service, are now relying heavily on public funding. Consequently, these services have to be accountable to the government and service-users. For every dollar and cent spent on a service, emphasis should be on efficiency and effectiveness. Nevertheless, when talking about evaluating the effectiveness of social services, one would argue that there are lots of changing variables that affect service delivery and service outcomes, to the point where it is difficult to predict accurate evaluation. Furthermore, these variables are complicated and mutually influencing, particularly in the context of working with the YAR. This is why it is not surprising to find many youth workers against service evaluation.

There are many reasons including individual, societal and cultural that account for the emergence of youth-at-risk. It would be difficult for social workers to change over a few months or a year the behaviours of many of these youngsters who have been manifesting such problems for over a decade or more. The Government has been adopting a paradoxical attitude in evaluating our services. When the youth crime rate decreases, the Government seldom mentions the efforts and good work of youth workers. But when youth crime rate is on the increase, the Government blames us for not making sufficient efforts and holding us accountable for the consequences. This is unfair![1]

Such comments may have its own justifications. Indeed by considering the complexities involved, measuring service effectiveness is not an easy task.

The effectiveness of a service means measuring the service output and outcome.. But can everything be measured? Measurement is generally thought of as the process of assigning labels to certain characteristics of things according to a set of rules. The "things" may be people (especially their thoughts, feelings, or reactions relevant to the practice situation), objects or events. The "rules" refer to steps for assigning labels in an explicit and consistent manner. Hudson (1978) proposed what he called the "first axioms of treatment", and these are: (a) if you cannot measure the client's problem, it does not exist, and (b) if a problem doesn't exist, that is, if you cannot measure the client's problem, you cannot treat it. Hudson stated these as universal propositions, then challenged us to refute them by citing concrete examples and exceptions.

The practice implications of Hudson's axioms are appropriate challenges to professional practices, especially with regards to measuring the effectiveness of services for YAR in the current situation. The questions to ask here are: Why do youth workers in general resist the concept and practice of service evaluation? Could services for the YAR be objectively and scientifically measured? Do methods employed in evaluating service effectiveness really reflect the true standard and performance of the service?

Service Evaluation of Outreaching Social Work Service

Evaluation of service provided for YAR in Hong Kong began in the mid-1980s. With the upsurge of juvenile crime in the late 1970s and early 1980s (Working Group on Juvenile Crime, 1981), lots of resources, money and manpower, were invested into programmes handling the problem of YAR, especially on OSW teams. But the complex problem — juvenile crime — the Government attempted to tackle did not disappear. The Government and public grew more cautious, as there was increasing pressure to provide evidence of the effectiveness of the YAR services in order to justify the allocation of limited resources to the services. With this backdrop in 1985, OSW service, being a subvented youth programme designed specially to serve the YAR, undertook its first evaluation. It has been unanimously agreed that when one talks about social welfare service for YAR, one is talking about the provision of OSW service. The OSW programme was formally implemented in June 1979 with the establishment of 18 OSW teams and 10 professionally trained social workers in each team addressing the needs of 18 priority communities. Its objective is to reach-out to, and establish contact with, young people in places where they are known to frequent, such as playgrounds, parks, fast-food restaurants, housing blocks and street corners. The objective was to render services to help these YAR to develop their potential through education or training, more stable employment and social integration and to help solve individual or group problems through counselling, guidance and other relevant services (Hong Kong Government, 1982). In 1985, the Government decided to commission an evaluation study of the service. Ng and Man of the Chinese University of Hong Kong had been commissioned to conduct the service evaluation of OSW. The main objective of the research was to evaluate the overall effectiveness of the entire service programme. The purpose of the research was to measure the outcome of the service programme and summative evaluation was employed. By considering the practicality of the study, the research team chose the multiple time series design and compared the significance of changes between a control group and an experimental group. The experimental group consisted of youth served by the then 18 OSW teams and the control group was made up of youth of similar demographic characteristics but without the intervention of the outreaching social workers. Three steps of data analysis were employed to analyze information collected from the Clientele Information System (CIS) forms submitted by the outreaching social workers. The first step was to compare mean score change of the experiential group and the control group in the review sequence. The second step was to apply T-test on comparison of the two groups on their review sequence and the third step was to use regression analysis. Content analysis was also employed for information gathered through visits to the OSW teams during the research period. Based on the data collected, the following conclusions were drawn:

> The effectiveness of out-reaching social work is measured by the successfulness of problem solution for the youths at risk. Results of data analysis on information gathered from the major instrument (CIS) show that out-reaching service has some effects in reducing youths' behavioural problems such as "gambling", "anti-social", "association with undesirable peers" and "poor family relationship". Out-reaching social workers are able to help clients develop their social skills, choose their career and constructively use their leisure time. Insufficient evidences are found on the effectiveness of out-reaching social work in the problems of drug, sex and truancy. The overall results of out-reaching social work, in comparison with the non-treatment for youths in the control group, is significantly effective as suggested by the regression analysis. ... Based on the information gathered and analysis made it is confirmed that youths in the out-reaching programme were, in general, curbed from further deterioration in their behaviour problems. Out-reaching social work programme were able to help youths reduce their gambling habits and anti-social behaviour. The out-reaching social workers were also quite successful in helping youths to disassociate with undesirable peers and provided them with opportunities for constructive leisure activities. Through which, youths were able to develop their social skills. They also were found having better relationship with their family and becoming more serious with

their career choice and working attitudes. However, out-reaching social work service has not been very successful in dealing with the problems of drug, sex and truancy for this group of youth (Ng and Man, 1985: 219).

Nevertheless, the limitations of such kind of service evaluation were also recorded in the Research Report: "The different constraints of evaluative research have been considered and the limitations of the present Study have also been discussed. ... It is unanticipated that the data collection methods met so many difficulties. ... The quick turnover of social work staff in the outreaching teams also attributed to the mishandling of the CIS forms. This is also accounted for some amount to data attrition. The major limitation of this study is the inability of the investigators to collect data directly from the outreach clients ... " (Ng and Man, 1985: 221).

After the 1985 study, no large-scale official service evaluation has since been conducted on OSW service. Taking into account the aims, work focus, approaches, target service recipients, etc, OSW service is an important and irreplaceable service for YAR. Hence when we talk about effectiveness of services for YAR, we are actually talking about the effectiveness of OSW service.

Since mid-1990, under the Funding and Services Agreement (FSA) contracted between the Social Welfare Department and the NGOs operating OSW teams, the service output of the teams must meet the performance standards in order to secure funding support. According to the FSA for OSW service, the service operators will have to meet the following performance standards:

Output standard	*Output Indicators*
1.	No. of cases (including potential cases) of a service unit[2] per month
2.	No. of cases closed, having achieved case goal plan of a service unit per year
3.	No. of clients identified through external contact and direct approach of a service unit per year.
4.	No. of direct contact hours of a service unit per year
5.	The service operators will meet the requirements of the 16 Service Quality Standards (SQSs).

The performance standards laid out in the FSA in evaluating the effectiveness of OSW service belong to the single system evaluation method elaborated by Thyer (1993). Single System Evaluation is the use of simple and outcome measurement designs (e.g. no. of cases handled, etc.) to evaluate practice, to help identify progress, make practice decisions and acts as an aid to accountability. Thyer wrote (1993: 96):

> Single system designs can be used to answer two very different types of questions, evaluative and experimental. The evaluation question is: Did the client system improve during the course of social work intervention? The experimental question is: Did the client system improve because of social work intervention?

Quality Improvement Process Model

Public confidence in and funding of OSW service are diminishing. The public is calling for more service accountability. We have entered into an evidence-based era in which only the best social service delivery programmes — which can demonstrate the provision of needed, useful and competent services for the clients — will survive.

How do we go about providing these services? We can employ the quality improvement process model as a guide. The process in this model is a philosophy. It is a commitment to continually look for and seek new ways to make the services we offer to clients more responsive, more efficient, and more effective, without losing our mission and aims. Quality improvement means that we continually monitor and adjust (when necessary) our practices, both at a practical and a programme level. In this model, evaluation is essential and necessary. It provides the basic tools for us to engage in the quality improvement process. Such quality improvement process provides answers to questions raised earlier: Is outreaching social work service worth doing? How do I know if I am doing well? Can human services like the OSW service be scientifically evaluated?

In the FSA of OSW service, the delivery of the service can be divided into two levels: case level and programme level. It is at the case level that workers provide services to clients as individuals, groups and communities. With these points in mind, a programme-level evaluation is nothing more than aggregations of case-level evaluations. To put it another way, case-level evaluations evaluate the effectiveness and efficiency of individual services, while programme-level evaluations evaluate the effectiveness and efficiency of the whole programme.

Advantages of Doing Service Evaluation

One of the basic aims in helping YAR is to help them know what to do for themselves. Knowing how to help them involves practitioners' possession of both practical skills and relevant knowledge. In this context, knowledge-based evaluations can be used in the quality improvement process in the following four ways:

- To gather data from the outreaching social workers in order to develop "theories" about youth problems, especially juvenile delinquency, school drop-outs and youth unemployment;
- To apply these developed "theories" in actual practice condition;
- To develop treatment interventions on the basis of actual programme operations, and
- To test treatment interventions in actual practice settings.

The second reason for doing evaluation to improve the quality of our service is to gather data in an effort to provide important information that will help decision makers at all levels. The stakeholders, people who make decisions from evaluation studies of OSW service, relies heavily on the information. Many kinds of decisions would have to be made such as the operations or modes of service delivery of the service, funding, administrative issues, modes of service delivery for enhancing service output and outcomes. Four stakeholder groups include Government (funder), concerned Legislative Counsellors, the general public and clients. These stakeholder groups need concrete and reliable data to make the most appropriate kind of decisions.

The third advantage of using evaluation for the quality improvement process is to demonstrate accountability. Demonstrating accountability, or providing justification of a service, is a legitimate evaluation purpose as it involves a genuine attempt to identify the service's strengths and weaknesses, opportunities and threats (SWOT).

The last advantage of evaluation in the quality improvement process is to determine and find out if clients are getting what they need from a social programme. Responsible outreaching social workers are interested in finding out to what degree their clients are satisfied with their services, and whether their service objectives have been achieved; that is, they are interested in evaluating their individual practices. Under such circumstances, service evaluation on service effectiveness is important.

Outreaching Social Work Service: An Art or a Science

For those who maintain that the evaluation of OSW service — or the evaluation of anything for that matter — is impossible, never really "objective", politically incorrect, meaningless and culture-biased, this belief is in itself philosophically biased. This is a socially constructed dichotomy that is peculiar in an industrial society. It leads to the unspoken assumption that a person is an "artist" or an "evaluator" but not both, and certainly not both at the same time. This addresses the same assumption held by many outreaching social workers: taking into account the nature and causation of the clients' problems, OSW service can never be scientifically measured! In many ways, they see themselves as "artists". Artists, as myth has it, are sensitive and intuitive people who are hopeless at mathematics and largely incapable of logical thought. Evaluators, on the other hand, who use "scientific research and evaluation methods", are supposed to be cool and insensitive creatures whose ultimate aim, some believe, is to reduce humanity to a scientific nonhuman equation.

Both of the preceding statements are absurd, but a few of us may, at some deep level, continue to subscribe to them. Some of us may believe that youth workers are artists who are warm, empathic, intuitive and caring. From such a perspective, the thought of evaluating a work of art does seem almost blasphemous. Some outreaching social workers, more subtly influenced by the myth, argue that evaluations using any evaluation methods do not produce results that are relevant in human terms. It is true that the results of some evaluations done to improve the quality of OSW service delivery system are not directly relevant to individual frontline practitioners and their clients. This usually happens when the evaluations were never intended to be relevant to those two groups of people in the first place. Perhaps the purpose of such an evaluation was to increase our knowledge base in a specific problem area, or perhaps the data were not interpreted and presented in a way that was helpful to the frontline practitioners who were employed by the programme. Nevertheless, the relevance argument goes beyond saying that an evaluation produces irrelevant data that spawn inconsequential information to frontline workers. It makes a stronger claim: Evaluation methods *cannot* produce relevant information because youth problems have nothing to do with numbers and "objective" data. In other words, evaluation, as a concept, has nothing to do with OSW practice.

Outreaching social workers are professional social workers, and in working with YAR, they are artists as well as scientists. They have to collect information and data to help guide various decision-making processes in an effort to produce more effective and efficient services to clients. Therefore, the art of OSW practice and the use of established evaluative methods to help improving the service quality coexist. Outreaching social workers can, in the best sense and at the same time, be both "caring and sensitive artists" and "hard-nosed evaluators". Evaluation (science) and art are not separated. They are interdependent and interlocked. They are both essential to OSW practice.

Myths and Fears of Service Evaluation

A myth that fuels resistance to the quality improvement process via evaluations is that an evaluation is a horrific event whose consequences should be feared. Many outreaching social workers may be afraid of an evaluation because it is them who are evaluated: it is their services that are being judged. They may be afraid for their jobs, their reputations, and their clients; or they may be afraid that their services will be curtailed, abandoned, or modified in some unacceptable way. They may also be afraid that the data from the evaluation may be misused. They may believe that they no longer control this data and that the client's confidentiality has been breached. These fears have some bases. Services are sometimes curtailed or modified as a result of an evaluation. However, it is rare for social services to be abandoned because of a negative evaluation, at least, in the case of the welfare sphere in Hong Kong, this has seldom happened. They are usually shut down because they are not doing what the funders intended, or they are not keeping up with the current needs of the community and continue to deliver antiquated service that the funding sources no longer wish to support, or are financially constricted to do so. They can also be terminated because of the political climate. On the other side of the coin, an evaluation may mean that a social service programme will be expanded or similar programmes put into place. It cannot be just the results and consequences of an evaluation that generate fear, it is the idea of being judged.

An evaluation of a social service programme conducted once every five years by an outside evaluator is traumatic. On the other hand, an ongoing evaluation mechanism can be built in by the practitioners themselves as a normal part of day-to-day operations and a routine part of the service delivery. The point is that "evaluation phobia" stems from a false view of what an evaluation necessarily involves.

The Current Development

With faith and rapid development of Integrated Children and Youth Services Centres (ICYSCs), which are thought to be a better mode of service delivery for youth services (SWD, 2002), the then 34 OSW teams, of various sizes in the territory were re-organized and re-structured into 16 District Youth Outreach Social Work Teams (YOTs), to serve in 13 districts of the territory. Basically, the operation approaches remain the same. In the past two decades, OSW service has only had one thorough service evaluation and the results were positive. The annual service review exercise of OSW/YOT service carried out by the Social Welfare Department based on the performance standards laid out in the FSA appears to be routine monitoring of the service. There has not been any explicit sanction i.e. subvention cut imposed on the teams due to negative evaluation results. In other words, the provision and evaluation of OSW/YOT service through the current mechanism has proven the service to be effective, at least, in being able to meet the standards of the government. Henceforth, the OSW/YOT workers must critically reflect on the intrinsic values and importance of service evaluation and its direct relation with quality improvement. Recognizing that service evaluation is a must, they should learn to do away with all the fears and myths associated with service evaluation.

Conclusion

We have so far discussed the two major reasons for why outreaching social workers resist the concept and practice of service evaluation, i.e. philosophical biases (myths) and fears. Despite the queries we have in the methods and outcomes of service evaluation, the reality confronting us is an era in which the evidence-based approach is accepted as the main thrust of service evaluation. Evaluation of service efficiency is closely tied in with the subvention system and this is increasingly being recognized as an essential feature in the service monitoring system. As professional social workers, we need to face this challenge with determination and make proactive efforts to participate in the evaluation process. The research report of Ng and Man (1985) stated clearly the merits of the OSW service, especially its effectiveness in reducing behavioural problems of young people such as gambling, anti-social behaviour, association with undesirable peers, and poor family relationships. OSW was proved to be able to help youngsters develop social skills, make appropriate career choices, and use their leisure time constructively.

Hong Kong society is experiencing serious problems in youth crime and youth unemployment today. Other than reducing the anti-social behaviour of the risky youth, two other significant areas of working with YAR are developing good communication between youth and their parents, and promoting constructive use of leisure time. While it is expected that there will be no further in-depth evaluation of the service in the near future, and assuming that the Social Welfare Department is satisfied with the output and outcome of OSW teams/YOTs, outreaching social workers must make their best efforts to help YAR through both casework and group work. Outreaching social workers must demonstrate with evidence that they are competent and effective in providing guidance to these young people in peers relationships, job selection and career development, family relationships, and correction of socially inappropriate behaviours. It is only with solid evidence that the Government would recognize the effectiveness of the service, and the irreplaceability of the service would then be enhanced. If this is achieved, service evaluation will no longer be seen as a threat, and OSW/YOT workers will not fear filling out the various forms for accountability; instead, clear and systematic reporting would only prove the cost-effectiveness of the service.

There is still much development prospect for the outreaching approach in children and youth work in Hong Kong, particularly in relation to youth unemployment which is an emerging domain full of challenges and opportunities. A number of scholars (Furlong, 1992; Evans & Heinz, 1994; Julkunen, 2001) reiterate that youth employment will become the most difficult problem to manage in the twenty-first century. If not properly handled, youth unemployment will spark off more serious juvenile delinquency, putting the youth and their families and the society in a disturbing disequilibrium. In Hong Kong, unemployed young people are drawing much attention from various sectors. Considering this context, it is high time that youth workers, especially outreaching social workers, make themselves ready to give evidence of the effectiveness of their work, in order to establish their credibility for handling youth unemployment and related issues.

Service evaluation and service effectiveness goes hand-in-hand. The fundamental reason for conducting service evaluation is to improve the quality of services. To conclude, service evaluation is a must because it: (1) helps increase our knowledge base; (2) helps guide decision making; (3) helps demonstrate accountability and (4) helps assure that the YAR are getting what they need.

OSW works. The integration of practice and evaluation to form an empirically based approach, represents the goal and strategy of achieving a practice that works, and a service that is effective. The ultimate mission of service evaluation in the field of human services is to assist in improving the quality of social programmes. Such mission will continue to exist and to promote the future development of human services.

9

Rethinking Youth Problems in a Risk Society:
Some Reflections on Working with "Youth-at-Risk" in Hong Kong

Sammy Wai-sang Chiu

Youth has long been a concern of the government and the social work profession in Hong Kong, both in terms of care and control. Despite the recent re-organization and restructuring of service at the district level, youth work remains one of the largest service areas in the terrain of social work in the SAR. Notwithstanding this, however, the history of youth work in Hong Kong was quite problematic , as young people were not guided properly, and were often construed as potentially destructive during their transition to adulthood. Youth identity as a target of state control and intervention has thus been securely constructed since the 1970s and continued to be reproduced without being challenged throughout the 1990s and beyond. Mok (1999) in his analysis of youth policy in Hong Kong contended that the Hong Kong Government attempted to construct three categories of youth identities accorded different policy strategies: the youth elites to be rewarded; the ordinary youth to be neglected; and the problem youth to be disciplined. As implied, the youth elites are the cornerstone of future economic success, but the problematic caused disruption to social stability and economic development. The elites are but a few, yet the problematic could be many. As far as social welfare policy for youth is concerned, the effort of the state is to ensure to the farthest extent, that young people in general and problem youth in particular, would not turn out to be disruptive if not destructive forces for the economy (Hong Kong Government, 1991).

Social work attention invested on the youth-at-risk reflects a continuation of the efforts of the state in disciplining young people. This chapter discusses the uncertainties and vulnerabilities of young people in a world order that is now coined a risk society (Beck, 1992,

1999 & 2000). It is contended that the risks young people in Hong Kong
have to face now are very much different from before. Risks have now
become structural consequences of modernity and global capitalism,
which is far beyond personal control. Life paths and life chances of
young people are increasingly uncertain and fragmented, and the
education — work — retirement life route, which social work has long
assumed and worked towards, has become structurally unrealistic for
many youths today. While risks and life hazards are more unpredictable
and life paths more fragmented on the one hand, coping with the
consequence of risks needs to be more individualised. Social welfare in
general, and youth work in particular, has helped to strengthen the
personal nature of risks and seemingly overlooked the whole world
context upon which risks are produced and have largely been
transformed. It is therefore suggested that the personal notion of youth-
at-risk construed in Hong Kong has to be reconsidered so that on the
one hand risks could be redefined along a structural line to include
structural disadvantages of youth that exist beyond personal control.
On the other hand, youth workers also need to address the risks of young
people beyond the scope of personal development and social control.

From Unattached to At-risk: Three Decades of Social Work Intervention

The policing of youth through social work is not a new invention. Hall
and Jefferson (1976) of the then Centre for Contemporary Cultural
Studies (CCCS) argued that youth (sub)culture specifically of the
working class has always been a subject of state control. It is also
through youth (sub)culture that class struggles and resistance are
displayed. The classical analysis of the development of youth service
in Hong Kong was seen through massive riots in the 1960s, setting a
good example of state policing. This needs no further elaboration. From
the 1970s onwards, policing of working class youth had continued to
develop alongside the expansion of youth work services, though the
faces of which were varied. The mushrooming of Children and Youth
Centres offered opportunities to govern the developmental path of young
people, in which youth were socialised to conformity, both in terms of
values and behaviour. To the then colonial government, youth were to
be developed to become responsible citizens (Hong Kong Government,
1981 & 1991), which in other words, was taken to mean developing
young people to become contributive to capital accumulation (Chiu,

2002). For those who failed to conform, special attempts were then needed to bring them back on the right track, which might also be the only available track to success

The attempts of the government in policing non-conforming youth through social work have reflected in the construction of various problem identities. In early 1970s, pioneering of detach work in some voluntary agencies called to attention help for working class youth, who in some cases, were seeking career development in street gangs. The notion of "risk" and "vulnerability" among youth were not seen in detach work, and the social and structural dimensions of risk appeared almost totally absent in its basic assumption and intervention rationale. Rather, the sense of youth-as-problem appeared to be more obvious, where in the early days of detach-work, the notion of youth-as-problem could be found more or less equivalent to the general notion of problem youth.

While Macdonald et al. (1993) usefully distinguished between the traditional notion of "youth as trouble" and the more liberal notion of "youth in trouble", and Griffin (1997) further contended that the former is usually used to refer to young men who are subject of social work and other forms of state intervention where the latter represents young women needing protection, the distinction seems nevertheless insignificant at least in detach-work. The pioneering of detach-work was nevertheless substantiated by social work research in the 1970s and 1980s, where the efforts to help the problem youth were formalised into the government plan of outreaching social work (Ng et al., 1975; Ng & Man, 1985; Hong Kong Government, 1981). Based primarily on control theory, Ng et al. (1975) concluded that young people would be more prone to crime if their attachment to conventional social institutions such as the family and school and their bonding to normal social values were weak. In order to prevent these young people from falling into delinquency and crime, outreaching efforts had to be developed to help the "unattached youth" to regain attachment to the family, school, and other normal networks. The thrust of outreaching social work was not merely for young people to stay physically in school and at home, but for them to develop positive relationships with the institutions and to seek satisfaction and approval within them. However, in operational terms, the identification of the "unattached" was bound to be difficult, and it would appear only possible through identifying behavioural categories as well as the physical settings in which young people clustered. Though not explicitly stated, the unattached youth in the 1980s represented mainly those young people who were more crime-prone but had not yet committed crime. In another popular discourse of the 1980s, they were the marginal youth who were at the margin of crime.

What is important to point out is that the discourse of marginal youth seemed not only to imply the marginal identity of some young people, but also to have set its focus on the person rather than on the problems that young people were facing. The notion of vulnerability was sometimes used alongside youth marginality to explicate, for example, the association with harmful peers and negative values system. However, the concept of youth vulnerability was only narrowly conceived to mean "vulnerable youth" rather than youth who are vulnerable to external disadvantages and risks. As pointed out by Shi (2001), vulnerability can be more appropriately viewed as a multidimensional construct and its prevalence goes far beyond personal factors. Wikstrom and Wikstrom (2001) also related vulnerability to the risks that people are exposed to. As far as vulnerability is concerned, risks that caused vulnerability are mostly identified to be external to the persons who are subject to vulnerability. While vulnerability and risks have almost been established as a twin-concept, Turner (2001) in a more recent study suggests further that the inherent risks of modernity has intensified risks and vulnerability in social life. Take the study of poverty as an example, Townsend (1981) in his classical study of poverty in the United Kingdom, began to adopt the concept of vulnerability in the discussion of poverty, where he suggested that older workers were more prone to risks of low-pay, marginalisation and loss of employment, and thus were more vulnerable to poverty. Again, Townsend's (1981) thesis also related vulnerability to social disadvantages caused by social changes. Because of the fact that vulnerability is external to the persons, intervention and help are thus called forth to remove as far as possible the social disadvantages that put people at risk. Nevertheless, notwithstanding the importance of recognising the social dimensions of vulnerability, working with unattached and marginal youth in Hong Kong seemed to remain primarily focused on tackling personal deficiency rather than social disadvantages. Although risk is inevitably linked with the vulnerability of youth, it was not being addressed beyond the scope and depth of personal problems.

As a matter of fact, an official government welfare document which pinpointed the issue of youth at risk and called forth corresponding social work attention only appeared in the 1990s. Ironically, though, it arose as a result of the review of the services of the Children and Youth Centre which took place in early 1990s, and a report of which was published in 1994 (Working Party on Review of Children and Youth Centre Services, 1994). The report and the subsequent operational manual suggested several priority areas of youth work, where addressing the problem of youth-at-risk was included as one important priority. In line with this service focus, the government had also set up, under the leadership of the Director of Social Welfare, a Committee on Services for Youth At Risk, which aims at facilitating multi-disciplinary, cross-sector, cross-bureau/department co-ordination and collaboration to enhance services for young people (Social Welfare Department, 2002). The Committee was given the objective of examining the emotional and social problems faced by young people as they grow up and to oversee and monitor services provided by various departments in addressing the problem of youth at risk. However, given the way the government conceived risks, confronting young people today appeared to be vague. From the problems being highlighted, such as emotional youth problems, drugs and substance abuse, violence and other behavioural problems, etc. it gives people an impression that the concern about youth-at-risk has become just another fashionable catchword of the 1990s, and its content does not differ much from concern about the unattached and the marginal youth in the 1970s and 1980s.

The Notion of Risk in Youth Work

"Risk" is not a self-explanatory concept. As a general description, risk has been customarily referred to as a neutral concept which encompasses the dual elements of "danger" and "opportunity". Theoretically therefore when a young person is at-risk, an opportunity is readily available. However, this is always an ideal rather than a reality. Douglas (1992) has noted that risk nowadays has gradually changed from a neutral term to a more specifically and narrowly negative concept where only negative outcomes are to be realistically anticipated. In outlining a conceptual continuum of youth at risk for counsellors, McWhirter et al. (1998) defines risk as fixed presumed cause-and-effect dynamics that place the youth in danger of negative "future events". The cause and effect method in defining youth-at-risk is echoed by Capuzzi and Gross (1996) who attempted to identify the risk factors in education. Interestingly, though the notion of risk has become primarily negative, it has been portrayed as an all-embracing youth experience to which every young person is equally susceptible (McWhirter et al., 1998). Colthart (1996) conceived risk as an almost natural product in the process of transition from youth to adulthood. As suggested by Colthart (1996), a young person is viewed as being at-risk if life circumstances threaten his/her physical, psychological or emotional well being and limit the normative developmental experiences necessary to achieve adult functioning. Similar to the suggestion of Colthart, Batten and Russell (1995) also conceptualised youth-at-risk along the theses of developmental psychology and argued that all youths are in some sense at-risk because of their psychological, physiological and "social stress and tensions" experienced during adolescence.

The attempt to conceptualise youth-at-risk in terms of developmental threats has served, though perhaps unintentionally, to dilute and obscure the social and structural dimensions of risks confronted by some particular groups of youth in the society. As pointed out by Kelly (2001) the view that all young people are potentially at-risk represents an attempt to regulate all youthful behaviour, which is very dangerous. Tait (1995 & 2000) further argued that the widespread discourse of youth-at-risk provides an instrument to govern youth behaviour and dispositions. While the discourse of risk legitimises the governmentality of youth, the process of producing the risk discourse is nonetheless endless (Tait, 1995). Burchell (1996) further argued that the developmental thesis of crisis has sought to individualise the risks of young people and to "responsibilise" them and their families for the conduct and consequences of individual biographies. In practice, social workers often find it more pragmatic to identify behavioural traits as well as the personal and family circumstances of young people as signs of risks, and to begin social work accordingly. For example, traits such as truancy, absenteeism, school drop-out, drug and alcohol abuse, gang clustering, violence and sexual abuse, night-drifting, school bullying, etc. are often regarded as red flags for at-risk youth (Aksamit, 1990; Barber and McClellan, 1987; Lee, 1997; Paulu, 1987; Wong; 1997). Capuzzi and Gross (1996) further identified such behaviours as "failing to obey rules or directives; avoiding taking part in family activities; arguing about everything, and displaying values and attitudes different from family, etc." as markers of youth at risk. While these behavioural and circumstantial markers are essentially useful to raise early signal for help, it would also be misleading if they eventually become the sole problem owned by the young people upon which intervention measures are to be formulated. In other words, when behavioural and circumstantial markers are taken to mean risks, efforts and attention to help youth-at-risk may easily be directed towards controlling and diminishing the signs instead of targeting the social disadvantages and vulnerability that caused these behavioural and circumstantial signs.

The problem with the personal orientation of working with youth at risk is that it tends to overlook that even personal and natural risks are socially caused. Blaike et al. (1994) in the study of natural hazards in the third world concluded that even natural disasters are not just natural events. Rather, they are the result of the social, political and economic environment which structures the lives of different groups of people. As pointed out by sociologists, risks, vulnerability and disadvantages are socially structured, and their distribution is not equal (Townsend, 1981; Caserta and Gray 1984; Schervish, 1983). For example, unemployment has very much to do with one's social class background and one's relative powerlessness in the labour market (Schervish, 1983). While unemployment is a significant factor leading to youth disadvantages, the risk of being unemployed is not equally distributed between class, age and gender. Another typical example is sexual violence, a fundamentally gendered issue which reflects the domination of male over female of different ages. It would be simplistic to conclude girls' risk to sexual violence as their own personal problems or behavioural misdoings.

In short, the risks that are confronting young people today are rooted in the social positions that young people are located. Risks are socially structured and their distribution varies according to one's social class, gender, and the relative power (or powerlessness) in the society. Behavioural and circumstantial markers are signs which signal the risk and the social disadvantages that young people are facing, but they are not problems by themselves. Instead of just tackling behaviour traits, social workers working with youth-at-risk must be aware of focusing their intervention on the social disadvantages and powerlessness caused by the class, gender and age structure of the society in order to be anti-oppressive. I shall return to this point in the final part of this chapter.

Rethinking Risks in a Risk Society

After analysing the background to the social production of risk confronting young people, it is necessary to situate the discussion of risk within the notion of risk society put forward by Giddens (1991 & 2000) and Beck (1992). In the past three decades we have enjoyed changes and developments that were by and large stable and predictable. The direction of change, as it appeared, was moving towards improvement of material living standard, education, social welfare, and not least, accumulation of wealth especially for the wealthy minority. Indeed, modernity, as vividly coined by sociologists, has brought about remarkable success in the economy and improvement of living standard in the industrial world, in which Hong Kong has been a part (Hoogvelt, 1997). We have developed a relatively stable economic system with capitalist mode of production in Hong Kong, and correspondingly, we have also developed a sophisticated social institution (also coined as mode of regulation), including education and welfare, so as to regulate the odds of the economic system. People of different ages and genders were structured into different roles and positions with different life paths. Individual variations inevitably existed, but the route was generally predictable. The perspective of youth work in Hong Kong has been shaped more or less within the "modernity project", where the life paths of young people and their corresponding roles and behaviours were framed according to the requirement of the economy. The education — work (or family) — retirement chain is so fixated that almost everyone in the society is expected to go through it without bypassing. Without exception, young people are expected to comply with this route and to conform to its underlying values.

With the route fixed, those who fail or refuse to follow it through for whatever reason, were offered help, remedies, and as a last resort, controlled.

However, we are witnessing a world that is undergoing unprecedented transformation. Beck (1992) suggested that the industrial society is now being replaced by a risk society, in which the old, stable, progressive and "scientific" world view is being challenged; predictabilities and certainties, characteristics of modernity, are threatened, and a new set of risks and opportunities are brought into existence. Giddens (1991 & 2000) contended that, unlike in modernity where risks were caused primarily by ignorance, personal failure or failure to master the environment, risks in "high modernity" is created by knowledge. In other words, risk is fundamentally a reflexivity of human advancement (Kaspersen, 2000). In the last few centuries, the advancement of knowledge and technologies have helped master the environment, control health and prevent other natural hazards. But modernity, including technological advancement and social institutions, has brought new environmental damage, new conflicts, as well as global and local deprivations. Unlike in the past, the uncertainties and risks we face now are beyond what human rationality can control and calculations can ensure. One example elicited by Beck (1992) is the over-cutting of forests due to industrialisation, which resulted in environmental damage to the whole world. In the past, health hazards were mostly related to undersupply of hygiene technology, but today it is closely related to overproduction in the industrial sector. Beck (1992) suggests that sooner or later problems and conflicts related to the distribution of wealth will be compounded by the distribution of risks. Along this line, Culpitt (1999) argued the distribution of risks is not at all an individual experience, and many a time it is still class- and gender-based. Globally as well as locally, as I have discussed in the earlier part of this chapter, the distribution of risks is always biased against the weak, the powerless and the deprived groups in the community. As argued by Beck (1992: 35)

> Like wealth, risks adhere to the class pattern, only inversely; wealth accumulates at the top, risks at the bottom ... Poverty attracts an unfortunate abundance of risks. By contrast, the wealthy (in income, power or education) can purchase safety and freedom from risk.

As such, the notion of risk society has not superseded the structural explanation of risk, but it has called forth social workers to look at youth-at-risk from an additional perspective. That is, beyond personal problems and structural disadvantages, risk has to be seen in addition, as a consequence of late modernity where it happens in the process of transformation of the economy.

New Risks Faced by Youth in a Risk Society

Fragmentation between the school and labour market

As pointed out vividly by Furlong and Cartmel (1997), many risks faced by young people today are actually unprecedented to the generation of their parents, and similarly, to the generation of their social workers. In the past, school leavers were expected to enter the labour market with paid employment, and could successfully do so without too much difficulty if they were serious in doing so. Education served as an instrument to differentiate and divide the labour force so that those who have different levels of education and vocational skills might enter into different layers of the labour market. From time to time there were youngsters who, for one reason or another, failed or refused to enter, yet the continuity between school and labour was by and large smooth, where transition from school to work was not too much a systemic problem. However, as a result of the restructuring of the labour market and the concomitant decline in the local economy, entry into the labour market for school leavers has been increasingly difficult. According to recent government statistics, labour participation rate of young people aged between 15-24 has significantly fallen from 48.5% in 1997 to 44.9% in 2001. In April 2002, the labour participation rate of youth sank to its lowest ever figure of 43% (Census and Statistics Department, 2002). On the other hand, youth has consistently been one of the most vulnerable age groups for unemployment over the past 5 years. It can be seen that involuntary worklessness, which can be regarded as discontinuity between school and the labour market, has become one of the major risks of young people today in Hong Kong. As suggested by Beck (2000), the distribution of the risk of being workless is not equally shared by all young people. Instead, this risk is most often centered at the bottom where the least educated usually suffer more seriously. Chiu and Wong (2000) in their study of youth unemployment in Taipo explained this as a process of "squeezing down", meaning that those with a higher education level have increasingly needed to take up jobs that are occupied by their less educated counterparts, and those with the lowest education and vocational skills are most at risk from being squeezed out from the labour market. What is important is that this is a systemic risk rather than one faced by individuals. The assumption that there is a smooth continuity between the education system and the labour market is now at stake. Instead, fragmentation has begun to appear where young people are losing out.

In addition, the response of the labour market towards restructuring also reflexively aggravates the risk faced by young people. In order to retain profitability in a highly competitive economy, Chiu (2002) argued that capitalists and employers in Hong Kong today are less willing to invest on training of young workers compared with the situation a few decades ago. Rather, young school leavers are often expected to mature readily and be able to perform well for profit making once having been employed. Unfortunately, the skills required for maturity in the economic and labour market are not taught in schools. The rigidity and lack of flexibility in the Hong Kong education system have not only brought about frustration for primarily lower class youth who perceive their careers differently, but more importantly, have further enlarged the gap between education and work and fragmented the life route which is fixed for every young person in society.

Another aspect of fragmentation between education and the labour market, that is unprecedented in the past, is the change of production mode. Instead of needing a stable and massive labour force for maximization of production, the economy now requires flexible, short-term labour for multi-tasking. This poses obvious difficulties for old age labour as it would almost be impossible to transform their knowledge and skills into multi-tasking ones. Similar disadvantages are faced by youth especially those school leavers without working experience. On the other hand, demand for flexible short-term labour also implies that seeking job advancement through traditional long-term career and stable employment methods, is outdated. There is an apparent fragmentation, if not conflict, between traditional work values and employment reality that young people are facing. Young people today have to face the risk of losing their jobs involuntarily. Certainly again, this happens more to the lower class, less educated and less skilled youth.

Inconsistency between production and consumption

In view of the decline of the local economy, government officials often simplified the problem as the lack of confidence in consumption. This is a typical assumption of consumer-led economic recovery, which suggests that once confidence in consumption is resumed the economy will naturally recover. Whether the logic of consumer-led recovery is workable is not a topic of concern here, but what the logic has implied is a new ethic of consumption (Bauman, 1998). In the past, a mature and responsible citizen has a duty to engage in economic production (work ethics). Now, there is an added duty to consume responsibly. Yet in order to stimulate consumption, the market has on the one hand strongly promoted the diversity of choice in consumer goods, while on the other hand, has enlarged the consumer sector by promoting consumption of different age groups such as the youth and the elderly. Four major risks have arisen out of this phenomenon.

Firstly, there is a gap between the ethic of work and the ethic of consumption. The former requires diligence and self-control (traditional ethics of being mature and responsible), whereas the latter relies on pleasure-seeking and self satisfaction. Striking a balance is very often possible in theory rather than in reality both for the adults and for young people.

Secondly, there is also an obvious gap between the ethics to consume and the ability to spend. While the ethic to consume has been so widely encouraged and penetrated into the lives of young people through mass and telecommunication media, their ability to spend, however, has been greatly limited by their position in the labour market. This problem is very obvious in Hong Kong where pop culture products and fashionable goods have been targeted on young people so as to enlarge their market size and profits. Young people are thus being placed in a risk position which they might not be able to cope with.

Thirdly, a state of value confusion exists when there is a gap between promoting responsible citizenship through production and the encouragement of consumption as a new duty. The traditional set of norms are still being upheld but is no longer able to address the real life situations of young people today, at least as far as the encouragement of consumption is concerned. While education and social work are agents which continue to strengthen the work ethics, the capitalist system has saliently transformed the traditional definition of responsible citizen through mass media and consumption. Young people are caught in the middle whereby their new set of behaviour socially produced by the ethics of consumption does not match with the old norms. This gap and the risk it created has brought about considerable strains on young people in Hong Kong society nowadays.

Finally, encouragement of consumption relies on diversity of choice, which in return creates the diversity of interests. However, on a day-to-day reality for young people, diversity of interests is but a myth that does not exist outside the realm of consumption. For example, the existing education system and its related reward and punishment mechanism has not been able to respond to the diversity of interests produced by the economic sector. Not only that the mode of primary and secondary education has remained unchanged, but the reward for success and failure remains centered around academic study rather than other abilities. In other words, diversity is required in work and in consumption, but diversity of interests and ability is not encouraged and accommodated in school.

Some Reflections for Social Work

Young people in Hong Kong today are facing new sets of risks that are brought about by the process of social and economic transformation. These new risks are mostly systemic which are beyond the control of individual young people. In view of this, social workers may need to reposition their own role and reconsider their practice which addresses the risks of young people in Hong Kong. There are several areas which warrant social workers' attention:

1. There is a need to reconceptualise so as to broaden the definition of youth-at-risk. As argued, risks are increasingly not personal

problems, but are failures or deficiencies in a risk society. They are more often reflexivity of our capitalist system. Young people are placed in risk positions but the system does not allow them to solve it. The risks are embedded in the capitalist system. Behavioural markers are useful in helping us identify who are in risk situations, but they are not systemic risks themselves.

2. Based on the reconceptualisation of risk, social workers should gradually initiate or at least participate in the redefinition of youth transition. After all, the old life route of education-work-retirement is not applicable to many young people today due to the fragmentation of work and discontinuity between education and work caused by the transformation of the economy. Structured by the new mode of economic production, it is necessary for some young people to go through multiple transitions from school to work. Definition of successful transition must be broadened to accommodate multiple transition.

3. Social workers need to address the risks created by the fragmentation of work and discontinuity between education and work. Government measures at present, for example, the youth work experience and training scheme, are symbolic rather than substantial. They either fall short of provision to adequately satisfy the needs of young people, or reproduce the discontinuity and fragmentation that exist between school and work. To address the problem of fragmentation and discontinuity, the government has a responsibility to negotiate with the commercial sector to jointly establish more apprentice schemes for young people. This approach has won considerable success in continental Europe because it benefits both the employers and the young people.

4. Social workers may consider working hand in hand with the education sector in gradually reformulating the reward mechanism in school with a view to encourage and reward more diversities of student ability. This measure not only helps respond to the requirements of the work system for multiple ability, but also helps reduce failures in school and thus reduces risks for young people when they fail to cope with the frustrations confronting them.

5. While diversities are being celebrated in economic production and consumption, diversity of interest and social values would inevitably emerge. Social workers may need to recognise the value changes and value confusion that young people and the society are facing, and thus to constantly re-adjust our scope of work in relation to the changes in society.

Conclusion

Social work in Hong Kong has gone through three decades of work with the street clusters, the unattached, the marginal and the at-risk. In a time of social and economic transformation, attention is called forth to address risks that are produced by the risk society. The concept of youth-at-risk needs to be expanded from inherent problem of young people to reflexive consequences of the capitalist system. The range of social work needs corresponding expansion to cover both containment of youth behavioural problems and promoting changes in social policies and in promoting social reforms.

10

Working with "Youth-at-risk":
The Way Ahead

Francis Wing-lin Lee

Different chapters have discussed the various approaches to working with YAR who have different problems. The approaches employed to work with YAR, to a large extent, depend on our understanding of the causes of their problems. There can be various perspectives on understanding youth problems/deviance. These include the physiological perspective (Glueck and Glueck, 1956; National Institute of Mental Health, 1970; Philpott, 1978), psychological perspective (Gerard, 1970; Hewitt and Jenkins, 1946; Inhelder and Piaget, 1958; Kohlberg, 1963; Piaget, 1948; Schoenfeld, 1975) and sociological perspective (Burgess, 1926; Cloward and Ohlin, 1960; Cohen, 1955; Durkheim, 1933; Merton, 1968; Morris, 1957; Park et al, 1925; Sutherland, 1939). Depending on which perspective one favours, the focus of intervention differs. In fact, studies have shown that youth problems are multi-causational (Kornhauser, 1978; Lee, 1993; Regoli and Hewitt, 2000) and are the results of the interaction of different social systems (e.g. family, school, peers, mass media) that the young people are subject to (Lee, 2002a). These imply the need for multi-level intervention to remedy and prevent the problem. The intervention scope basically includes the individuals, the peers, the families, the schools and the communities.

Different individual and group methods to work with YAR or youth gangs have been suggested (Capuzzi and Gross, 1996; Chan et al., 1997; Klein, 1971; Lam, 1997; Lee, 1994a & 2000; Lee et al, 1996; Lo, 1986, 1992 & 1993; Spergel, 1995). In terms of working with YAR on an individual level, one idea that deserves more attention has been promoted by Lee and Cham (2002). This is the idea of "user (client) participation". In their study, they discovered that, contrary to ordinary views that would think that YAR are immature, with a low self-image, lack of communication skills, unable to cope with stress and lack of control (Dryfoos, 1990; Jessor et al., 1991; McWhirter et al., 1998), they can participate in the helping process if they are given chances. The study intensively interviewed 15 juvenile delinquents (JDs) and 15 social workers (SWs) who worked with the delinquents. It found the JDs were quite ready to participate in the helping process, while the SWs also saw positive growth of their clients through their participation in the helping process. User participation in this study mainly connotes service users' (clients') active participation in assessing their problems and needs, formulating the intervention plans for themselves and evaluating the effectiveness of the intervention with the workers. Three main conclusions of the study are that: (1) successfully helping YAR is not mainly determined by workers' good will, genuineness, sensible advice, concern and resources; (2) the provision of opportunities for active participation of clients in the helping process is important; and (3) active participation includes expressing opinions, asking questions, making choices, sharing information, and working together with workers (Lee and Cham, 2002).

Lee (1990) has proposed the conception of the criminalization process in understanding the gradual engagement of YAR in delinquency/crime. He suggested that subject to different unfavourable influences, YAR would gradually engage in different kinds of delinquency if no appropriate interventions/services are provided in the process. The young delinquents would end up becoming hard core adult criminals if the situation does not improve. He further introduced the concept of intermediate intervention into the criminalization process of the YAR (Lee, 1990). This concept is similar to the concept of early intervention to the YAR, that is to offer some kind of intervention/ service to the YAR before his or her engagement into the delinquent/ criminal career deepens (Figures 1 & 2) (Lee, 1996). The idea of immediate intervention should be adopted as a direction for working with YAR. In fact the concept and methods of intermediate intervention have been quite popular in the United Kingdom (Curtis, 1989; Ray and Kerslake, 1979).

The approaches employed by intermediate intervention to YAR, which the author favours, include three main components: (1) it uses individual guidance work and group guidance work methods as in social work; (2) it is a community-based intervention and (3) it emphasizes developing positive aspects of the young people (de-labeling). From a meso-level, it emphasizes the need of district cooperation and

Criminalization Process

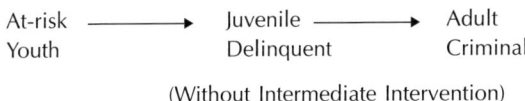

(Without Intermediate Intervention)

Figure 1 Criminalization Process of YAR without Intermediate Intervention

Criminalization Process

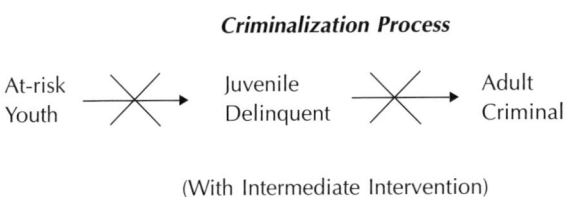

(With Intermediate Intervention)

Figure 2 Prevention of Criminalization Process of YAR with Intermediate Intervention

coordination among concerned organizations, such as the social welfare services, police and schools. In fact, the need to promote district cooperation and coordination between social services and police has been advocated (Lee, 1994b & 2002b).

It has been pointed out that young people face similar developmental needs and problems. It is only due to their different social realities and limitations that they have employed different means of adaptation and adjustment for satisfying their needs and resolving their problems. To classify some groups of young people as YAR is only for the convenience of designing models of service delivery. We should see the YAR as youth in general who, only due to their unique social situations, have exhibited difficulties in tuning into our general societal life. They need services to satisfy their needs, resolve their problems and enhance their living (Lee, 1994a: 36).

With this conception in mind, one would agree that the receiving of services for assisting their positive growth and development is a right of the YAR. So, to intervene in the situations (problems) of the YAR as an intermediate intervention is the correct move.

Adolescence is a transition period from childhood to adulthood. With the same logic, the problems of adolescents are also transitional.

In order to help prevent YAR from becoming adult criminals, prevention and early intervention (with similar ideas as intermediate intervention) are significant. We also need to identify the risk and protective factors for young people to commit delinquency (Tang and Davis, 1997). McWhirter et al. (1998) support the ideas of prevention and early intervention of YAR, and they have put forward some continuums illustrating the process of prevention/early intervention and treatment work (Figure 3) (McWhirter et al., 1998: 206).

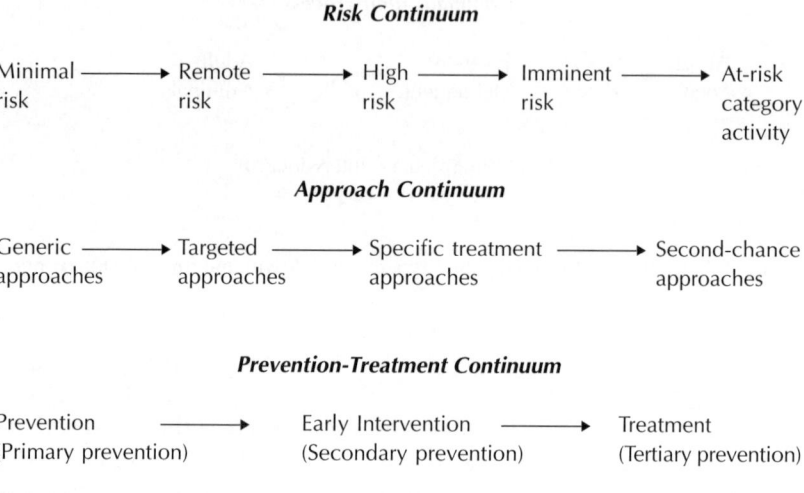

Risk Continuum

Minimal ——→ Remote ——→ High ——→ Imminent ——→ At-risk
risk   risk   risk   risk   category
                                                                        activity

Approach Continuum

Generic ——→ Targeted ——→ Specific treatment ——→ Second-chance
approaches   approaches   approaches   approaches

Prevention-Treatment Continuum

Prevention ————→ Early Intervention ————→ Treatment
(Primary prevention)   (Secondary prevention)   (Tertiary prevention)

Figure 3 Risk Approaches and Prevention Continuums (McWhirter et al., 1998)

They suggested that young people with favourable social backgrounds (e.g. from families of high socioeconomic status, attending good schools, having love and caring relationships with families and friends, etc.) are assumed to be at minimal risk for future trouble. Young people with more unfavourable demographic characteristics (e.g. families of low socioeconomic status, members of minority groups, etc.) are positioned in the remote risk category. High-risk youth are those from unfavourable social backgrounds with dysfunctional families and schools coupled with personal negative attitudes, emotions and behaviours with deficit social skills and coping behaviours. Young people in the imminent risk category basically shared the same characteristics with the high-risk youth, but in addition, exhibit more gateway behaviours and activities (e.g. aggression, alcoholism, etc.). Young people belonging to the at-risk category basically have all the characteristics of young people in the previous 4 categories. They have further engaged in, what can be regarded literally as, delinquent behaviours, such as dropping-out of schools, abusing substances, etc. (McWhirter et al., 1998: Chapter 1).

As illustrated in Figure 3, different approaches are applicable for different parts between the risk continuum. For example, generic approaches, that imply the conducting of some general delinquent prevention programmes such as life-skills, decision-making and problem-solving skills training, can be run for young people in the minimal risk and remote risk categories in a community. Targeted approaches are aimed at young people situated in or between the remote risk and high risk categories. They are more vulnerable to committing delinquency. Tailor-made programmes should be conducted for these young people with reference to the problems/potential problems they are exposed to. Specific-treatment approaches are located for those between high risk and imminent risk categories. As young people in these categories might have actually exhibited some problematic/ delinquent behaviours, the design of specified treatment programmes should address problems such as alternative and coping behaviours to family problems, stopping abusing substances, and staying in schools, etc. Finally, the second-chance approaches are for those who have already engaged in problematic activities, such as dropping-out of schools, abusing substances, pregnancy, etc., due to bad choices. They should be given a second chance or opportunity to improve their situation (McWhirter et al., 1998: Chapter 11).

Conceptually, McWhirter et al. (1998) used primary prevention (prevention), secondary prevention (early prevention) and tertiary prevention (treatment) to signify different phases and levels of intervention. The core programmes for prevention and early intervention to YAR proposed by McWhirter et al. (1998) include life-skills training, interpersonal communication skills training, strategies for cognitive change (Rose, 1998) and stress coping skills training.

The causes of problems for young people are multiple. We need to understand them from multi-levels and a system perspective (Lee, 2002a). Prevention and early intervention with appropriate programmes tailor-made for the needs of YAR are believed to be the right approaches for tackling the problems. "To prevent is better than to cure!"

Notes

CHAPTER 3

1. As at March 2003, there were 34 Outreaching Social Work Teams serving 34 priority areas with relatively higher juvenile crime rate and youth population in the territory.
2. These 30 OR teams had been serving in the prioritized communities for more than one year at the time of study. It is believed that one-year service experience was basic for a team to develop an appropriate work system for its workers to follow.
3. Originally, an experienced worker (with more than three-years of service experience) from each of the 30 OR teams was invited for the interview. However, only 19 teams responded energetically.
4. In working with youth gangs, OR workers will design particular treatment goals for particular gangs with reference to their particular assessed needs. Effective or successful intervention means the treatment goals designed have been achieved.

CHAPTER 5

1. See *Hong Kong Standard*, April 10, 1998; *Oriental Daily*, June 2, 1999; *Ming Pao*, February 5, 1999.
2. See *Oriental Daily*, May 19, 1997.
3. See *Ming Pao*, February 14, 1999.
4. See *Sing Tao Daily*, September 18, 2001.
5. A whole school approach is widely known in the field of education. For more information, please see:
    — Rogers, B. (1995). *Behaviour Management: A Whole-School Approach.* London: Paul Chapman Publishing Ltd.
    — Humm J., & I. Mocroft (2001). *Bully-Proofing a School.* London: Community Development Foundation.

— Arora, C.M.J. (1994). Is there any point in trying to reduce bullying in secondary schools? *Educational Psychology in Practice*, Vol. 10, No. 3, 155–162.

6. This centre is a non-profit making organization, which is very active in anti-bullying movement in recent years.

CHAPTER **8**

1. Comments from a youth worker in a sharing session.
2. A service unit refers to a unit which the subvention is allocated at the snapshot. The size of units may vary while a full team should comprise of 10 social workers.

References

PREFACE

Commissioner of Police (1993). *Royal Hong Kong Police Review 1992.* Hong Kong: Government Printer.

—— (1994). *Royal Hong Kong Police Review 1993.* Hong Kong: Government Printer.

—— (1995). *Royal Hong Kong Police Review 1994.* Hong Kong: Government Printer.

—— (1996). *Royal Hong Kong Police Review 1995.* Hong Kong: Government Printer.

—— (1997). *Royal Hong Kong Police Review 1996.* Hong Kong: Government Printer.

—— (1998). *Hong Kong Police Review 1997.* Hong Kong: Government Printer.

—— (1999). *Hong Kong Police Review 1998.* Hong Kong: Government Printer.

—— (2000). *Hong Kong Police Review 1999.* Hong Kong: Government Printer.

—— (2001). *Hong Kong Police Review 2000.* Hong Kong: Government Printer.

—— (2002). *Hong Kong Police Review 2001.* Hong Kong: Government Printer.

Cohen, R.K. (1955). *Delinquent Boys: The Culture of the Gang.* New York: Free Press.

Dryfoos, J.G. (1990). *Adolescents At Risk: Prevalence and Prevention.* Oxford: Oxford University Press.

Glueck, S. and Glueck, E. (1956). *Physique and Delinquency.* New York: Harper.

McWhirter, J.J., McWhirter, B.T., McWhirter, A.M. and McWhirter, E. H. (1998). *At-Risk Youth: A Comprehensive Response.* (could the title be A Comprehensive Response?) (2/e) N. Y.: Brooks/Cole Publishing Company.

Morris, T. (1957). *The Criminal Area: A Study in Social Ecology.* U. K.: Routledge and Kegan Paul.

Schoenfeld, C.G. (1975). A Psychoanalytic Theory of Juvenile Delinquency. In People, E. E. (ed.) *Readings in Correctional Casework and Counseling.* CA: Goodyear: 24–6.

Sutherland, E.H. (1939). *Principles of Criminology.* (3/e) Philadelphia: Lippincott.

李永年 (編著) (2002). 香港青少年問題 - 廿一世紀初的現象、剖析與對策。香港大學出版社。[Lee, F.W.L. (ed.) (2002). [*Hong Kong Youth Problems in the Early 21ˢᵗ Century — The Phenomena, Analyses and Solutions.* Hong Kong: HKU Press.]

CHAPTER 1

Aberdeen Outreaching Social Work Team (Caritas-HK); Eastern District Outreaching Social Work Team (NAAC), Shau-Chai Outreaching Social Work Team (CYMCA) & Central and Western District Outreaching Social Work Team (HKYWCA) (2000). *Report on Study of Substance Abuse Behaviours of Young People in Discos and Rave Parties.* (in Chinese).

Au, C.F. (1997). *Youth in Hong Kong: A Statistical Profile 1997.* Hong Kong: Commission on Youth.

Capuzzi, D. and Gross, D.R. (eds.) (1996). *Youth at Risk: A Prevention Resource for Counselors Teachers and Parents.* (2/e) VA: American Counseling Association.

Cheung Sha Wan Children and Youth Integrated Service Centre, Boys' and Girls' Clubs Association of Hong Kong (1999). *Report on Study of Young People Participation in Activities of Youth Gangs.* (in Chinese) Hong Kong: Boys' and Girls' Clubs Association of Hong Kong

Cheung, Y.W. (1997). Family, School, Peer, and Media Predictors of Adolescent Deviant Behavior in Hong Kong. *Journal of Youth and Adolescence.* Vol. 26(5): 569–95.

Commissioner of Police (1999). *Hong Kong Police Review 1998.* Hong Kong: Printing Department.

—— (2000). *Hong Kong Police Review 1999.* Hong Kong: Printing Department.

—— (2001). *Hong Kong Police Review 2000*. Hong Kong: Printing Department.

Dryfoos, J.G. (1990). *Adolescents At Risk: Prevalence and Prevention*. Oxford: Oxford University Press.

Ho, B. (1985). *Royal Hong Kong Police Force*. (in Chinese) Hong Kong: Hoi Shan Publishing Company.

Hong Kong Federation of Youth Groups (1993). *The Push and Pull Factors of Joining Juvenile Gangs*. (in Chinese) Hong Kong: Hong Kong Federation of Youth Groups.

—— (1999). *Report on the Phenomenon and Tendency of Dropout (Draft for Press Conference)*. (in Chinese) Hong Kong: Hong Kong Playground Association. *Hong Kong Standard* (10.4.1998). (Newspaper)

Hugh-Jones, S. and Smith, P.K. (1999). Self-reports of short- and long-term effects of bullying on children who stammer. *British Journal of Educational Psychology*. 69: 141–58.

Jessor, R., Donovan, J.E. and Costa, F.M. (1991). *Beyond Adolescence: Problem Behavior, and Young Adult Development*. New York: Cambridge University Press.

Lee, F. (1994). Group Work with "Youth-at-risk". *Asia Pacific Journal of Social Work*. Vol. 4(2): 31–40.

Lee, F.W.L., Lo, T.W. and Wong, D.S.W. (1996/97). Intervention in the Decision-making of Youth gangs. *Groupwork*. Vol. 9(3): 292–302.

Lo, T.W. (1984). *Gang Dynamics*. Hong Kong: Caritas-Hong Kong.

—— (1992). Groupwork with Youth Gangs in Hong Kong. *Groupwork*. Vol. 5(1): 58–71.

—— (1993) Neutralisation of Group Control in Youth Gangs. *Groupwork*. Vol. 6(1): 51–63.

Luk, W.K. (2002). Three or Five in a Gang — Phenomenon of Youth Gangs. In Lee, F.W.L. (ed.) *Youth Problems in Hong Kong: Phenomena, Analyses and Solutions in the Early 21st Century*. (in Chinese) Hong Kong: University of Hong Kong Press, 19–30.

McWhirter, J. J., McWhirter, B. T., McWhirter, A. M. and McWhirter, E. H. (1998). *At-Risk Youth: A Comprehensive Response* (2/e) N. Y.: Brooks/Cole Publishing Company.

Ming Pao (14.2.1999). (Chinese Newspaper)

Narcotics Division, Government Secretariat, HKSAR, PRC (2000). *Central Registry of Drug Abuse: Forty-sixth Report (Jan. 1991 — Jun. 2000)*. Hong Kong: Printing Department.

—— (2001). *Central Registry of Drug Abuse: Forty-eighth Report (Jan. 1992 — Jun. 2001)*. Hong Kong: Printing Department.

—— (2002). *Central Registry of Drug Abuse: Forty-ninth Report (1992–2001)*. Hong Kong: Printing Department.

Olweus, D. (1993). *Bullying at School: What We Know and What We Can Do*. Oxford: Blackwell.

—— (1994). Bullying at school: basic facts and effects of a school based intervention programme. *Journal of Child Psychology and Psychiatry*. 35(7): 1171–90.

Oriental Daily (19.5.1997). (Chinese Newspaper).

—— (17.6.2000). (Chinese Newspaper).

—— (31.7.2000). (Chinese Newspaper).

Rigby, K. (1996). *Bullying in Schools: And what to do about It*. London: Jessica Kingsley Publishers.

Shing Pao (27.8.2000). (Chinese Newspaper).

Sing Tao (27.8.2000). (Chinese Newspaper).

—— (18.9.2001). (Chinese Newspaper).

Smith, P.K. and Sharp, S. (eds.) (1994). *School Bullying: Insights and Perspectives*. London: Routledge.

Smith, P.K. and Thompson, D. (eds.) (1991). *Practical Approaches to Bullying*. London: David Fulton.

Sun (27.8.2000). (Chinese Newspaper).

Sun Pao (27.8.2000). (Chinese Newspaper).

Vagg, J., Bacon-Shone, J., Gray, P., and Lam, D., (1995). *Research on the Social Causes of Juvenile Crime*. Hong Kong: University of Hong Kong.

Wong, S.W. and Lo, T.W. (2001). Preliminary Report on Study of School Bullying in *Secondary Schools*. (in Chinese) Hong Kong: Department of Applied Social Studies, City University of Hong Kong.

Wong, S. W., Lok, D., Lo, T.W., and Ma, S., (2001). *Preliminary Report on Bullying* against Schools: the Potential for Anti-bullying Programmes in Primary *School*. (in Chinese) Hong Kong: City University of Hong Kong.

CHAPTER 2

Clear, T.R. and Dammer, H.R. (2000). *The Offender in the Community*. California: Wadsworth.

Commission of Inquiry (1967). *Kowloon Disturbances 1966 – Report of the Commission of Inquiry 1967*. Hong Kong: Government Printer.

Coordinating Committee on Outreaching Social Work Service (1989). *Operational Manual for Outreaching Social Workers*. Hong Kong: Children & Youth Division, Hong Kong Council of Social Service.

Health, Welfare and Food Bureau/Social Welfare Department (June 2003). *Update on Measures to support Young People.* (Paper for Social Welfare Advisory Committee) (SWAC Paper No. 08/03).

Hong Kong Police Force (1995). *The Police Discretion Scheme.* (leaflet) Hong Kong: Government Printer.

Lee, F.W.L. and Tang, C.S.K. (1999). *Evaluation Study of Youth Mobile Team Service for Young Night Drifters.* Hong Kong: Authors.

Lo, K.M. (ed.) (1998). *Phoenix Spreads the Wings: Readings on Community Support Service Scheme.* (in Chinese) Hong Kong: Methodist Bookstore.

Lo. T.W., Wong, S.W., Chan, W.T., Leung, S.K., Yu, C.S. and Chan, C. K. (1997). Research on the Effectiveness of Rehabilitation Programmes for Young *Offenders.* Hong Kong: Government Printer.

McWhirter, J. J., McWhirter, B. T., McWhirter, A. M. and McWhirter, E. H. (1998). *At-Risk Youth: A Comprehensive Response.* (?) (2/e) N. Y.: Brooks/Cole Publishing Company.

Methodist Centre (2000). *Leaflet.* Hong Kong: Methodist Bookstore.

Ming Pao (Chinese newspaper) (29.5.2000).

Social Welfare Department (1998). *The Five Year Plan for Social Welfare Development in Hong Kong – Review 1998.* Hong Kong: Government Printer.

—— (2002). *A New Strategy to Support Young People – An Overview of Youth Welfare Services.* Hong Kong: Government Printer.

Vagg, J., Bacon-Shone, J., Gray, P. and Lam, D. (1995). *Research on the Social Causes of Juvenile Crime.* Hong Kong: University of Hong Kong.

Working Group on Juvenile Crime (1981). *Report of the Working Group on Juvenile Crime.* Hong Kong: Government Printer.

Working Party on Review of Children and Youth Centre Services (1994). *Report on Review of Children and Youth Centre Services.* Hong Kong: Government Printer.

Youth Outreach (2001). *Youth Outreach Annual Report - 2001.* Hong Kong: Youth Outreach.

Youth Outreach website: <http: //www.hkhoho.com/youthoutreach/index.htm>.

CHAPTER 3

Cartwright, D.S. (1975). The Nature of Gangs. In Cartwright, D.S.; Tomson, B. and Schwartz, H. (eds.) *Gang Delinquency.* California: Brooks/Cole: 1–22.

Casey, R.D. and Cantor, L. (1983). Group Work with Hard-to-Reach Adolescents: The Use of Member Initiated Program Selection. *Social Work with Groups*. Vol. 6(1): 9–22.

Collins, N. and Hoggarth, L. (1977). *No Man's Landmarks* (Report 6). U. K.: National Youth Bureau.

Cooper, C.N. (1967). The Chicago YMCA Detached Workers: Current Status Of An Action Program. In Klein, M. W. (ed.) *Juvenile Gangs in Context: Theory, Research and Action*. N. J.: Prentice-Hall: 183–93.

Editorial Committee on Outreach Journal (ed.) (1985). "Group Work". *Outreach Journal*. (in Chinese) No.7.

Fashimpar, G.A. and Harris, L.T. (1987). Social Work at 30 MPH: Mini-Bike Rehabilitation Groups for Juvenile Delinquents. *Social Work with Groups*. Vol. 10(1): 33–48.

Feldman, R.A. (1985). Group Work with Antisocial Youths. In Sundel, M.; Glasser, P.; Sarri, R. and Vinter, R. (eds.) *Individual Change Through Small Groups*. (2/e) N. Y.: Free Press: 473–93.

Garland, J.A., Jones, H.E. and Kolodny, R.L. (1973). A Model for Stages of Development in Social Work Groups. In Bernstein, S. (ed.) *Explorations in Group Work: Essays in Theory and Practice*. U. S. A.: Milford House: 17–71.

Goetschius, G.W. and Tash, M.J. (1967). *Working with Unattached Youth*. London: Routledge & Kegan Paul.

Goldstein, A.P. and Huff, C.R. (eds.) (1993). *The Gang Intervention Handbook*. Ill.: Research Press.

Klein, M.W. (1971). *Street Gangs and Street Workers*. N. J.: Prentice-Hall.

Lee, F. (1994). Group Work with "Youth-at-risk". *Asia Pacific Journal of Social Work*. Vol. 4(2): 31–40.

Lee, F.W.L., Lo, T.W. and Wong, D.S.W. (1996/97). Intervention In The Decision-Making of Youth Gangs. *Groupwork*. Vol. 9(3): 292–302.

Li, M.C. (1990). Group Work With Marginal Youth: A Case Study Of A Volunteer Group. In Social Welfare Manpower & Training Committee, HKCSS. (ed.) *Casebook of Social Work Intervention 1990*. H. K.: HKCSS: 16–27.

Lo, T.W. (1992). Groupwork With Youth Gangs In Hong Kong. *Groupwork*. Vol. 5(1): 58–71.

Luk, W.K. (2002). Three or Five in a Gang — The Phenomenon of Youth Gangs. In Lee, F.W.L. (ed.) *Youth Problems in Hong Kong: The Phenomena, Analyses and Solutions in the 21ˢᵗ Century*. (in Chinese). Hong Kong: Hong Kong University Press: 19–30.

MacDonald, J. (1980). Detached Youth Work in the Late 1960s and the 1970s: a Review of Work in Inner London. In Booton, F. and Dearling, A. (eds.) *The 1980s and Beyond: The Changing Scene of Youth and Community Work*. U. K.: National Youth Bureau: 143–55.

Marks, K. (1977). *Detached Youth Work Practice in the Mid-Seventies* (Occasional Paper 18). U. K.: National Youth Bureau.

Morse, M. (1965). *The Unattached*. U. K.: Penguim Books.

Pawlak, E.J. and Vassil, T.V. (1980). Prestructing Cooperation among Acting-out Youth. *Social Work with Groups*. Vol. 3(1): 31–40.

Pollio, D.E. (1995). Hoops Group: Group Work with Young "Street" Men. *Social Work with Groups*. Vol. 18(2/3): 107–22.

Smith, C.S., Farrant, M.R. and Marchant, H.J. (1972). *The Wincroft Youth Project: A Social-Work Programme in a Slum Area*. London: Tavistock.

Spergel, I.A. (1965). *Street Gang Work: Theory And Practice*. Mass.: Addison-Wesley.

—— (1995). *The Youth Gang Problem: A Community Approach*. N. Y.: Oxford University Press.

Thrasher, F.M. (1927). *The Gang: A Study of 1,313 Gangs in Chicago*. Chicago: University of Chicago Press.

Witt, P.A. and Crompton, J.L. (eds.) (1996). *Recreation Programs that Work for At-Risk Youth: The Challenge of Shaping the Future*. Pennsylvania: Venture Publishing, Inc.

CHAPTER **4**

Action Committee Against Narcotics (2002). *Report on Narcotics in Hong Kong — 2002*. (in Chinese) Hong Kong: Government Printer.

Beck, J.E. and Rosenbaum, M. (1994). *Pursuit of Ecstasy — The MDMA Experience*. New York: State University of New York.

Booth, D.J. (1997). *Drugspeak — The Analysis of Drug Discourse*. University of Strathelyde, UK: Harwood Academic Publishers.

Caritas Aberdeen OSW Team, NAAC Eastern OSW Team, CYMCA Chai Wan OSW Team, HKPA WC/NP OSW Team, and HKYWCA C & W OSW Team (2000). Report of A Study on Substance Abuse of Young People in Discos and Rave *Parties*. (in Chinese) Hong Kong: The Four Teams.

Committee on Substance Abuse, HKCSS (2000). *Report of A Study on Party Substance Abuse*. (in Chinese). Hong Kong: HKCSS.

Denning, P. (2000). *Practicing Harm Reduction Psychotherapy: An Alternative Approach to Addictions.* New York: Guilford Press.

Ettorre, E.M. (1989). Women and Substance Use/Abuse: Towards a Feminist Perspective or How To Make Dust Fly. *Women's Studies International Forum.*

—— 12(6): 593–602.

—— (1992). *Women and Substance Use.* London: Macmillan.

—— (1995). *Gendered Moods: Psychotropic and Society.* London: Routledge.

Freedman J. and Combs G. (1996). *Narrative Therapy: The Social Construction of Preferred Realities.* USA: W.W. Norton & Company.

Hammersley, R., Khan, F. and Ditton, J. (2002). *Ecstasy and the Rise of the Chemical Generation.* New York: Routledge.

Harm Reduction Coalition (2001). *Principles of Harm Reduction:* USA. <www.harmreduction.org>

Ho, Wing-yin Cecilia (2001). *Conception and Practice of Drug Use: The Case of Female Adolescents in Rave Party and Disco in Hong Kong.* (MSW Dissertation) Hong Kong: Department of Social Work, Hong Kong Baptist University.

Holland, J. (ed.) (2001). *Ecstasy: The Complete Guide: A Comprehensive Look at the Risks and Benefits of MDMA.* Rochester, Vermont: Park Street Press.

Hong Kong Christian Service (2000). *Report of A Study on Deconstructing Party Drug Abusers.* (in Chinese) Hong Kong: HKCS.

Hong Kong Council of Social Service (2000). *Abstract of Report of Case Study on Substance Abuse of Northbound Youth from Hong Kong.* (in Chinese) Hong Kong: HKCSS.

Hong Kong Narcotics Division (2003). *Press Release.* (Issued on 19 December 2003).

Hong Kong Narcotics Division (2004). *Press Release.* (Issued on 9 June 2004).

Inciardi, J.A. and Harrison, L.A. (2000). *Harm Reduction: National and International Perspectives.* New York: Sage Publications, Inc.

Inciardi, J.A., Lockwood, D. and Pottieger, A.E. (1993). *Women and Crack-Cocaine.* London: University of Delaware, Macmillan Criminal Justice Series.

Leary, T.F. (1998). *The Politics of Ecstasy.* Berkeley, California: Ronin Publisher.

Lee, T.S. (2001). *Report on an In-depth Study of Psychotropic Substance Abuse in Hong Kong.* Hong Kong: Narcotics Division, Government Secretariat (Task Force on Psychotropic Substance Abuse).

Outreaching Service, Hong Kong Playground Association (2000). *Report of A Study on Substance Abuse of Young People in Discos/Rave Parties.* (in Chinese) Hong Kong: HKPA.

Redhead, S. (ed). (1993). *Rave off — Politics and Deviance in Contemporary Youth Culture.* (Popular Cultural Studies 1) Great Britain: Avebury, Athenaeum Press Ltd.

Rosenbaum, M. (2002a). *Safety First: Reality-Based Approach to Teens, Drugs and Drug Education.* San Francisco: Drug Policy Alliance.

—— (2002b). Ecstasy: America's New "Reefer Madness"? *Journal of Psychoactive Drugs.* 34(2): 137–42.

Sands, R. and Nuccio, K. (1992). Postmodern Feminist Theory and Social Work. *Social Work.* 37(6): 134–40.

Schur, Edwin M. (1994). *Labeling Women Deviant: Gender, Stigma, and Social Control.* New York: Random House.

Silverman, D. (2000). *Doing Qualitative Research — A Practical Handbook.* London: SAGE Publications Ltd.

South, Nigel (ed.) (1999). *Drugs — Cultures, Controls and Everyday Life.* London: Sage Publications.

Suffet, F. and Brotman, R. (1976). Female Drug Use: Some observations. *The International Journal of Addictions.* 11(1): 19–33.

Szasz, T.S. (1992). *Our Right to Drugs: The Case for a Free Market.* New York: Praeger Publishers.

Vastag, B. (2001). Ecstasy experts want realistic messages. *Journal of the American Medical Association.* 286(7): 22–36.

Zinberg, N.E. (1984). *Drug, Set and Setting: The Basis for Controlled Intoxicant Use.* New Haven, CT: Yale University Press.

CHAPTER **5**

Aberdeen Caritas Outreaching Team & Wong, S.W. (2000). *Report on School Bullying Behaviours in South District.* (in Chinese) Hong Kong: South District Council.

Arora, C.M.J. (1994). Is there any point in trying to reduce bullying in secondary schools? *Educational Psychology in Practice.* 10(3): 155–62.

Baldry, A.C. and Farrington, D.P. (2000). Bullies and delinquents: personal characteristics and parental styles. *Journal of Community and Applied Social Psychology.* 10: 17–31.

Besag, V. E. (1989). *Bullies and Victims in Schools.* Milton Keynes: Open University Press.

Bodine, R.J. and Crawford, D.K. (1998). *The Handbook of Conflict Resolution Education: A Guide to Building Quality Programmes in Schools*. San Francisco: Jossey-Bass Publishers.

Boulton, M.J. (1996). Bullying in mixed sex groups of children. *Educational Psychology*. 16(4): 439–43.

Byrne, B. (1999). Ireland. In Smith, P.K., Morita, Y., Junger-Tas, J., Olweus, D., Catalano, R. & Slee, P. (eds.) *The Nature of School Bullying*. London: Routledge, 112–27.

Cheung, Y.W. and Ng, A. (1988). Social Factors in Adolescent Deviant Behavior in Hong Kong: An Integrated Theoretical Approach. *International Journal of Comparative and Applied Criminal Justice*. 12(1): 27–45.

Chow, W.S., Tang, Y.M. and Chan, T.F. (1985). *A Study of the Values, Leisure, Behavior and Misbehavior of the Youth in Tsuen Wan and Kwai Chung*. Hong Kong: Tsuen Wan District Board.

Cowie, H. and Sharp, S. (1994). Tackling bullying through the curriculum. In Smith, P.K. and Sharp, S. (eds.) *School Bullying: Insights and Perspectives*. London, New York & Canada: Routledge, 84–107.

Education Department (1991). *Surveys on Unruly and Delinquent Behavior of Pupils in Secondary Schools*. Hong Kong: Government Printer.

—— (1993). *Review on Surveys on Unruly and Delinquent Behavior of Pupils in Secondary Schools*. Hong Kong: Government Printer.

Elliott, M. (ed.) (1997). *Bullying: A Practical Guide to Coping for Schools*. London: Pitman Publishing.

Farrington, D. (1993). Understanding and preventing bullying. In Tony, M. (ed.), *Crime and Justice: A Review of Research — Vol. 17*. Chicago: University of Chicago Press, 381–458.

Glover, D. and Cartwright, N. with Gleeson, D. (1998). *Towards Bully-free Schools: Interventions in Action*. Buckingham: Open University Press.

Harachi, T.W., Catalano, R.F. and Hawkins, J.D. (1999). United States. In Smith, P.K., Morita, Y., Junger-Tas, J., Olweus, D., Catalano, R. and Slee, P. (eds.) *The Nature of School Bullying*. London: Routledge, 279–295.

Hong Kong Standard, (April 10, 1998). (Newspaper)

Hugh-Jones, S. and Smith, P.K. (1999). Self-reports of short- and long-term effects of bullying on children who stammer. *British Journal of Educational Psychology*. 69: 141–58.

Humm, J. and Mocroft, I. (2001). *Bully-proofing a School*. London: Community Development Foundation.

Law, C.K. (1986). *A Study on the Behaviors and Attitudes of Youth in Kwun Tong*. Hong Kong: Kwun Tong District Board.

Limper, R. (2000). Cooperation between parents, teachers, and school boards to prevent bullying in education: An overview of work done in the Netherlands. *Aggressive Behavior*. 26: 125–35.

McCarthy, P., Sheehan, M. and Wilkie, W. (Eds.) (1996). *Bullying: From Backyard to Boardroom*. Australia: Millennium Books.

Mellor, A. (1999). Scotland. In Smith, P.K., Morita, Y., Junger-Tas, J., Olweus, D., Catalano, R. & Slee, P. (eds.) *The Nature of School Bullying*. London: Routledge, 91–111.

Ming Pao, (February 5, 1999). (Chinese newspaper)

—— (February 14, 1999). (Chinese newspaper)

Olweus, D. (1978). *Aggression in the Schools: Bullies and Whipping Boys*. Washington, D.C: Hemisphere Press.

—— (1993). *Bullying at School: What We Know and What We Can Do*. Oxford: Blackwell.

—— (1994). Bullying at school: basic facts and effects of a school based intervention programme. *Journal of Child Psychology and Psychiatry*. 35(7): 1171–90.

Ortega, R. and Lera, M.J. (2000). The Seville anti-bullying in school project. *Aggressive Behavior*. 26: 113–23.

O'Moore, M. (2000). Critical issues for teacher training to counter bullying and victimization in Ireland. *Aggressive Behavior*. 26: 99–111.

Oriental Daily, (May 19, 1997). (Chinese newspaper)

—— (June 2, 1999). (Chinese newspaper)

Peterson, L. and Rigby, K. (1999). Countering bullying at an Australian secondary school with students as helpers. *Journal of Adolescence*. 22: 481–92.

Perry, D.G., Kusel, S.J. and Perry, L.C. (1988). Victims of peer aggression. *Developmental Psychology*. 24: 807–14.

Rigby, K. (1996). *Bullying in Schools: And what to do about It*. London: Jessica Kingsley Publishers.

—— (1999). Peer victimization at school and the health of secondary school students. *British Journal of Educational Psychology*. 69: 95–104.

Rogers, B. (1995). *Behaviour Management: A Whole-School Approach*. London: Paul Chapman Publishing Ltd.

Roland, E. (2000). Bullying in school: Three national innovations in Norwegian schools in 15 years. *Aggressive Behavior.* 26: 135–43.

Salmivalli, C. (1999). Participant role approach to school bullying: implications for interventions. *Journal of Adolescence.* 22: 453–59.

Sharp, S. (1996). The role of peers in tackling bullying in schools. *Educational Psychology in Practice.* 11(4): 17–22.

Sharp, S. and Thompson, D. (1994a). The role of whole-school policies in tackling bullying behavior in school. In Smith, P.K. & Sharp, S. (eds.) *School Bullying: Insights and Perspectives.* London: Routledge, 57–83.

—— (1994b). How to establish a whole-school anti-bulling policy. In Sharp, S. and Smith, P.K. (eds.) *Tackling Bullying in your School.* London: Routledge, 23–40.

Siann, G., Callaghan, M., Glissov, P., Lockhart, R. and Rawson, L. (1994). Who gets bullied? The effect of school, gender and ethnic group. *Educational Research.* 36(2): 123–34.

Sing Tao Daily, (September 18, 2001). (Chinese newspaper)

Smith, P.K. (1999). England and Wales. In Smith, P.K., Morita, Y., Junger-Tas, J., Olweus, D., Catalano, R. and Slee, P. (eds.) *The Nature of School Bullying.* London: Routledge, 68–90.

Smith, P.K., Morita, Y., Junger-Tas, J., Olweus, D., Catalano, R. and Slee, P. (1999). *The Nature of School Bullying: A Cross-national Perspective.* London: Routledge.

Smith, P.K. and Sharp, S. (eds.) (1994). *School Bullying: Insights and Perspectives.* London: Routledge.

Smith, P.K. and Thompson, D. (eds.) (1991). *Practical Approaches to Bullying.* London: David Fulton.

Stephenson, P. and Smith, D. (1989). Bullying in the junior school. In Tattum, D. and Lane, D. (eds.) *Bullying in Schools.* Stoke-on-trent: Trentham Books, 45–57.

Sullivan, K. (2000). *The Anti-bullying Handbook.* Auckland: Oxford University Press.

Tattum, D. (ed.) (1993). *Understanding and Managing Bullying.* Oxford: Heinemann Educational.

Tattum, D. and Tattum, E. (1996). Bullying: a whole school response. In McCarthy, P., Sheehan, M. and Wilkie, W. (eds.) *Bullying: From Backyard to Boardroom.* Australia: Millennium Books, 13–23.

Vagg, J., Bacon-Shone, J., Gray, P. and Lam, D. (1995). *The Final Report on the Social Causes of Juvenile Crime.* Hong Kong: The University of Hong Kong.

Whitney, I., Rivers, I., Smith, P.K. and Sharp, S. (1994). The Sheffield project: methodology and findings. In Smith, P.K. & Sharp, S. (eds.) *School Bullying: Insights and Perspectives*. London: Routledge, 20–56.

Wong, S.W. (1998). Longitudinal Case Study on the Deviation Process of Youth-at-risk (in Chinese). *Hong Kong Journal of Social Work*. 32(1): 83–9.

—— (1999a). Culturally Specific Causes of Delinquency: Implication for Juvenile Justice in Hong Kong. *Asia Pacific Journal of Social Work*. 9(1): 98–113.

—— (1999b). A Case Study of Girl Delinquency in Hong Kong (in Chinese). *Journal of Youth Studies*. 2(2): 177–86.

—— (2001a). Pathways to Delinquency in Hong Kong and Guangzhou (South China). *International Journal of Adolescence and Youth*. 10 (1& 2): 91–115.

—— (2001b). *Harmony Schools vs. School Bullying — A Comprehensive Study in Wong Tai Sin District*. (in Chinese) Hong Kong: Wong Tai Sin District Fight Crime Committee.

—— (2001c). *The Problem of School Bullying in North District*. (in Chinese) Hong Kong: North District Council.

—— (2002). "Restorative Justice and Mediation Services". In W.L. Lee (ed.), *Youth Problems in Hong Kong in the Early 21st Century*. (in Chinese) Hong Kong: Hong Kong University Press, 151–63.

Wong, S.W., Lee, W.L. and Lo, T.W. (1995). *A Study of Youth Behaviors and Values in Tuen Mun: An Analysis of the Road to Deviance*. (in Chinese) Hong Kong: Tuen Mun District Board.

Wong, S.W. and Lo, T.W. (2001). *Preliminary Report on Study of School Bullying in Secondary Schools*. (in Chinese) Hong Kong: Department of Applied Social Studies,CityUHK.

Wong, S.W., Lok, D, Lo, T.W. and Ma, S. (2001). *Preliminary Report on Bullying against Schools: the Potential for Anti-bullying Programmes in Primary School*. (in Chinese) Hong Kong: City University of Hong Kong.

CHAPTER **6**

Austin, J., Joe, J.K., Krisberg, B. and Steele, P. (1990). *The Impact of Juvenile Court Sanctions: A Court that Works*. San Francisco, CA.: National Council on Crime and Delinquency.

Austin, J.K., Johnson, D. and Gregoriou, M. (2000). *Juveniles in Adult Prisons and Jails: A National Assessment*. Washington D.C., U.S. Dept. of Justice.

Angus, D.I. (2000). *Juvenile Delinquency: A Step in the Right Direction* (M.Soc.Sc. in Criminology Thesis, University of Hong Kong). Hong Kong: University of Hong Kong.

Backes, O. (1995). Diversion and Constitutional Crime Policy. *Diversion and Informal Social Control*. G. A. Wolfgang Ludwig-Mayerhofer. Berlin, Walter De Gruyter: 345–51.

Census and Statistics Department (2001). *Hong Kong Annual Digest of Statistics*. Hong Kong: Government Printer.

—— (2002). *Hong Kong Annual Digest of Statistics*. Hong Kong: Government Printer.

—— (2003). *Hong Kong Annual Digest of Statistics*. Hong Kong: Government Printer.

Chong, W.K.S. (2000) *The Police Cautioning Diversion Scheme: Participant Observation of Post-Caution Visits in Hong Kong*. (M. Phil. Thesis, University of Hong Kong). Hong Kong: University of Hong Kong.

Correctional Services Department (2001). *Annual Statistical Tables on Receptions*. Hong Kong: Government Printer.

Ezell, M. (1995). Measurements of Net Widening. *Diversion and Informal Social Control*. G. A. Wolfgang Ludwig-Mayerhofer. Berlin, Walter De Gruyter: 259–69.

Feld, B.C. (1999). The In re Gault Revisited: A Cross-State Comparison of the Right to Counsel in Juvenile Court. In Feld, B. (ed.) *Readings in Juvenile Justice Administration*. New York: Oxford University Press, P.117–26.

Fight Crime Committee (1996). *Annual Report*. Hong Kong: Government Printer.

—— (1996). *Annual Report*. Hong Kong: Government Printer.

—— (1997). *Annual Report*. Hong Kong: Government Printer.

—— (1998). *Annual Report*. Hong Kong: Government Printer.

—— (1999). *Annual Report*. Hong Kong: Government Printer.

—— (2000). *Annual Report*. Hong Kong: Government Printer.

—— (2001). *Annual Report*. Hong Kong: Government Printer.

—— (2002). *Annual Report*. Hong Kong: Government Printer.

Gray, P. (1991). Juvenile Crime and Disciplinary Welfare. In Traver, H. and Vagg, J (eds.). *Crime and Justice in Hong Kong*. H. K.: Oxford University Press, (P.25–41).

—— (1996). The Struggle for Juvenile Justice in Hong Kong 1932–1995. *Hong Kong Law Journal*. 26(3): 301–20.

—— (1997) The Emergence of the Disciplinary Welfare Sanction in Hong Kong. *The Howard Journal.* 36(2): 187–208.

Horwitz, A.V. (1995). Diversion and A Sociological Theory of Social Control. *Diversion and Informal Social Control.* G. A. Wolfgang Ludwig-Mayerhofer. Berlin, Walter De Gruyter: 17–34.

Joe Laidler, K. and Loh, C. (2002). *Project X: An Evaluation of an Early Intervention Program.* (Report to the Tuen Mun Project X Group) Hong Kong: Centre for Criminology, University of Hong Kong.

Krisberg, B. and Austin, J. (1993). *Reinventing Juvenile Justice.* Newbury Park, CA: Sage.

Lo, T.W., Wong, S.W. and Maxwell, G. (2003). *Measures Alternative to Prosecution for* Handling Unruly Children and Young Persons: Overseas Experiences and *Options for Hong Kong.* (A Study commissioned by the Security Bureau, HKSAR Government) Hong Kong: City University of Hong Kong.

Matthews, R. (1995). The Diversion of Juveniles from Custody: The Experience of England and Wales 1980–90. *Diversion and Informal Social Control.* G. A. Wolfgang Ludwig-Mayerhofer. Berlin, Walter De Gruyter: 83–104.

Muncie, J. (1999). *Youth and Crime.* London: Sage.

Provisional Legislative Council — Panel on Security, Subcommittee on Overcrowdedness In Penal Institutions (1997). *Minutes of the Meeting held on Thursday, 6 November 1997 at 2: 30 pm in Conference Room B of the Legislative Council Building.* http://www.legco.gov.hk/yr97–98/english/panels/se/opi/minutes/op061197.htm (accessed 8/4/04)

Schur, E. (1973). *Radical Non-Intervention.* Englewood Cliffs, NJ: Prentice Hall.

Schwartz, I. (1989). *Justice for Juveniles.* Lexington, D.C.: Heath and Company.

—— (1995). The Impact and Role of Juvenile Diversion in the United States. *Diversion and Informal Social Control.* G. A. W. Ludwig-Mayerhofer. Berlin, Walter De Gruyter: 75–82.

Spooner, C., Hall, W. and Mattick, R. (2001). An Overview of Diversion Strategies for Australian Drug Related Offenders. *Drug and Alcohol Review.* 20(3): 281–94.

Tuen Mun Fight Crime Committee (1999). *Special Issue on Project X.* (in Chinese) Hong Kong: Tuen Mun Fight Crime Committee.

Tuen Mun Project Group (1998). *Juvenile Crime: An Outlook for Tuen Mun.* (in Chinese) Hong Kong: Tuen Mun Fight Crime Committee.

CHAPTER 7

Bynum J. E. and Thompson W.E. (1992). *Juvenile Delinquency: A Sociological Approach.* (2/e) New York: Allyn and Bacon.

Cheung, Y.W. (1993). *Predicting Adolescent Deviant Behavior in Hong Kong: A Comparison of Media, Family, School and Peer Variables.* Hong Kong: Hong Kong Institute of Asia-Pacific Studies, The Chinese University of Hong Kong.

Cheung, Y.W. and Ng., A. (1988). Social Factors in Adolescent Deviant Behavior in Hong Kong: An Integrated Theoretical Approach. *International Journal of Comparative and Applied Criminal Justice.* 12: 27–45.

Elliott, D.S., Huizinga, D. and Ageton, S.S. (1985). *Explaining Delinquency and Drug Use.* Beverly Hill: Sage Publications.

Hirschi, T. (1969). *Causes of Delinquency.* Los Angeles: University of California Press.

Jang, S.J. and Smith, C.A. (1997). A Test of Reciprocal Causal Relationships among Parental Supervision, Affective Ties, and Delinquency. *Journal of Research in Crime and Delinquency.* 34: 307–36.

John, P. (1999). *Working with Young Offenders.* (2/e) London: Macmillan Press Ltd.

Krohn, N.D., Lizotte, A.J., Thornberry, T. P., Smith, C.A. and McDowall, D. (1996). Reciprocal Causal Relationships Among Drug Use, Peers, and Belies: A Five- wave Panel Model. *Journal of Drug Issues.* 26: 405–28.

Lam, D.O.B. (1998). Social Causes of Juvenile Crime. (in Chinese) *Journal of Youth Studies.* Vol. 1(2), Hong Kong: The Hong Kong Federation of Youth Groups.

Lee, F.W.L. (1996). *Teens of the Night: A Study on Night Drifting Young People in Hong Kong.* Hong Kong: Department of Social Work, The Chinese University of Hong Kong.

Lee, K.M. (2001). *The Impacts of Community Support Service Scheme on Young Offenders: A Case Study of Project Phoenix.* (M.Soc.Sc. Dissertation) Hong Kong: The University of Hong Kong.

Lo, T.W., Wong, S.W, Chan, W.T., Leung, S.K., Yu, C.S. and Chan, C.K. (1997). Research on the Effectiveness of Rehabilitation Programmes for Young *Offenders: Full Report.* Hong Kong: City University of Hong Kong.

Methodist Centre (2000). *Leaflet.* Hong Kong: Methodist Bookroom.

Ng, A.M.C., Lau, T.S., Lu, A., Tsoi, R. and Wong, K.H. (1975). *Social Causes of Violent Crimes Among Young Offenders in Hong Kong.* Hong Kong: Social Research Centre, Chinese University of Hong Kong.

Social Welfare Department (1994). *Information Paper on Community Support Service Scheme (CSSS).* Hong Kong: Government Printer.

—— (2000). *Funding Service Agreement of Community Support Service Scheme.* Hong Kong: Government Printer.

—— (2002a). *Information Paper on Referral Mechanisms for CSSS.* Hong Kong: Government Printer.

—— (2002b). *A New Strategy to Support Young People — An Overview of Youth Welfare Services.* Hong Kong: Government Printer.

Thornberry, T.P. (1987). Toward an Interactional Theory of Delinquency. *Criminology.* 25(4): 863–91.

Thornberry, T.P., Lizotte, A.J., Krohn, M.D., Farnworth, M. and Jang, S.J. (1991). Testing Interactional Theory: An Examination of Reciprocal Causal Relationships among Family, School, and Delinquency. *The Journal of Criminal Law and Criminology.* 82(1): 3–35.

Trojanowicz, R.C. and Morash, M. (1992). *Juvenile Delinquency: Concepts and Control.* (5/e) New Jersey: Prentice Hall.

Weis, J.G., Crutchfield, R.D. and Bridges, G.S. (1996). *Juvenile Delinquency (Volume 2 of Crime and Society).* U.S.A.: Pine Forge Press.

Yalom, I.D. (1985). *The Theory and Practice of Group Psychotherapy.* New York: Basic Books.

黃成榮、李永年及盧鐵榮 (1995). 《屯門區青少年行為問題研究：剖析青少年步向越軌青少年的新取向》。香港：屯門區議會出版。

黃成榮 (1997). 《危機青少年之越軌過程：個案追蹤研究報告》. 香港：基督教信義會北區外展社會工作隊。

黃成榮 (1999).《青少年價值觀及違規行為探索》。 香港：三聯書店。

盧錦華 (1998). 《鳳凰展翅 —— 社區支援服務文集》。香港：椒道衛理書室。

盧錦華及金明 (1994). 《火鳳凰 —— 再生的故事》。香港：椒道衛理書室。

盧錦華、李冠美及呂慧敏 (2001). 《展翅上騰 —— 探索先導青少年服務新路向》。香港：椒道衛理書室。

CHAPTER **8**

Alter, C. and Evens, W. (1990). *Evaluating your Practice: A guide to Self-assessment.* New York: Springer.

American Psychological Association. (1973). *Ethical Principles in the Conduct of Research with Human Participants.* Washington, DC: Author.

Austin, M.J. and Crowell, J. (1985). Survey research. In R.M. Grinnell, Jr. (Ed.), *Social Work Research and Evaluation.* (2/e) Itasca, IL: F.E. Peacock Publishers, (Pp. 275–305).

Babbie, E. (1992). *The Practice of Social Research.* (6/e) Belmont, CA: Wadsworth.

Bloom, M., Fischer, J. and Orme, J. (1994). *Evaluating Practice: Guidelines for the Accountable Professional.* (2/e) Englewood Cliffs, NJ: Prentice-Hall.

Blythe, B.J. and Tripodi, T. (1989). *Measurement in Direct Practice.* Thousand Oaks, CA: Sage.

Evans, K. and Heinz, W. R. (1994). *Becoming Adults in the 1990s*. London: Anglo German Foundation.

Furlong, A. (1992). *Growing Up in a Classless Society? School to Work Transitions*. Edinburgh, Scotland: University of Edinburgh Press.

Grinnell, R.M., Jr. (Ed.). (1997). *Social Work Research and Evaluation: Quantitative and Qualitative Approaches*. (5/e) Itasca, IL: F.E. Peacock Publishers.

Gilgun, J. (1997). Case designs. In R.M. Grinnel, Jr. (Ed.), *Social Work Research and Evaluation: Quantitative and Qualitative Approaches*. (5/e) Itasca, IL: F.E. Peacock Publishers, (Pp. 298–312).

Greenwald. R.A., Ryan, M.K. and Mulvihill, J.E. (1982). *Human Subjects Research*. New York: Plenum Press.

Hong Kong Government (1982). *Programme Plan on Personal Social Work among Young People*. Hong Kong: Government Printer.

Hudson, J., Mayne, J. and Thomlison R. (1992). (Eds.), *Action-oriented Evaluation in Organizations*. Middletown, OH: Wall & Emerson.

Hudson, W. W. (1978). First axioms of treatment. *Social Work*, 23, 65–66.

Julkunen I. (2001). Individual Strategies and Job Chances — A Comparative Perspective. *European Journal of Social Work*, Vol. 4 (3): 275–89.

Ng, A. and Man, P. (1985). *The Report on the Evaluation of Outreaching Social Work*. Hong Kong: Centre for Hong Kong Studies, The Chinese University of Hong Kong.

Social Welfare Department (2002). *A New Strategy to Support Young People — An Overview of Youth Welfare Services*. Hong Kong: Government Printer.

Thyer, B. A. (1993). Single-system research designs. In R. M. Grinned, Jr (Ed.). *Social Work Research and Evaluation*. Itasca, IL: Peacock, (pp. 94–117).

Working Group on Juvenile Crime (1981). *Report of the Working Group on Juvenile Crime*. Hong Kong: Government Printer. 2 A service unit refers to a unit which the subvention is allocated at the snapshot. The size of units may vary while a full team should comprise of 10 social workers.

CHAPTER **9**

Aksamit, F.L. Jr. (1990). "Mildly handicapped and at-risk students: the graying of the line" *Academic Therapy*. Vol. 25: 277–89.

Barber, L. and McClellan, M. (1987). "Looking at America's dropouts" *Phi Delta Kappan*. Vol. 69: 264–67.

Batten, M. and Russell, J. (1995). *Students At Risk: A Review of Australian Literature 1980–1994*. Melbourne: Australian Council for Educational Research.

Bauman, Z. (1998). *Work, Consumerism and the New Poor*. Buckinghamshire: Open University Press.

Beck, U. (1992). *Risk Society: Towards a New Modernity*. London: Sage.

—— (1998). "Politics of risk society" In J. Franklin (ed.) *The Politics of Risk Society*. Cambridge: Cambridge University Press, pp 9–22.

—— (1999). World Risk Society. Cambridge: Polity Press.

—— (2000). *The Brave New World of Work*. Cambridge: Polity Press.

Blaike, P., Cannon, T., Davies, I. and Wisner, B. (1994). *At Risk: Natural Hazards, People's Vulnerability and Disasters*. London: Routledge.

Burchell, G.. (1996). "Liberal government and the techniques of the self" In A. Barry, T. Osborne & N. Rose (eds.) *Foucault and Political Reason*. London: UCL Press.

Capuzzi, D. and Gross, D. (1996). "Defining youth at risk" In D. Capuzzi and D. Gross (eds.) *Youth At Risk: A Prevention Resource for Counselors, Teachers, and Parents*. Alexandria, VA: American Counseling Association, pp 3–19.

Caserta, M. and Gray, R. (1984). *Social Class, Vulnerability, and Depression among Hospitalized Utah Women*. Western Social Science Association Paper. Salt Lake City: Western Social Science Association.

Census and Statistics Department (2002). Statistics on Labour Force, Unemployment and Underemployment. <http: //www.info.gov.hk/ censtatd/eng/hkstat/fas/labour/ghs/labour1_index.html>

Chiu, S. (2002). "The prospects of youth work in Hong Kong". F.W.L. Lee (ed.) *Hong* Kong Youth Problems in the Early 21st Century — The Phenomena, Analyses *and Solutions*. Hong Kong: Hong Kong University Press. (In Chinese)

Chiu, S. and Wong, V. (2000). "Youth Unemployment in Hong Kong: Constraints and Social Policy Prospects" *Social Policy and Social Work*, Vol. 4(2): 91–126.

Colthart, A. (1996). "At risk youth participation in sports and recreation" *Youth Studies Australia*. Vol. 15(4): 31–7.

Culpitt, I. (1999). *Social Policy and Risk*. London: Sage.

Douglas, M. (1992). *Risk and Blame — Essays in Cultural Theory*. London: Routledge.

Furlong, A. and Cartmel, F. (1997). *Young People and Social Change: Individualization and Risk in Late Modernity*. Buckinghamshire: Open University Press.

Giddens, A. (1991). *Modernity and Self Identity: Self and Society in the Late Modern Age*. Cambridge: Polity Press.

Giddens, A. (2000). *Runaway World: How Modernization is Reshaping our Lives*. London: Routledge.

Griffin, G. (1997). "Representation of the young" In J. Roche and S. Tucker (eds.) *Youth in Society*. London: Sage, pp 17–35.

Hall, S. and Jefferson, T. (eds.) (1976). *Resistance Through Rituals : Youth Subcultures in Post-war Britain*. Hutchinson in association with Centre for Contmeporary Cultural Studies, University of Birmingham.

Hong Kong Government (1981). *Social Welfare into the 1980s* (White Paper). Hong Kong: Government Printer.

—— (1991). *Social Welfare into the 1990s and Beyond* (White Paper). Hong Kong: Government Printer.

Hoogvelt, A. (1997). *Globalisation and the Postcolonial World: The New Political Economy of Development*. Basingstoke, Hampshire: Macmillan Press

Kaspersen, L. (2000). *Anthony Giddens: An Introduction to a Social Theorist*. Oxford: Blackwell.

Kelly, P. (2001). "Youth at risk: process of individualisation and responsibilisation in the risk society" *Discourse: Studies in the Cultural Politics of Education*. Vol. 22(1): 23–33.

Lee, F.W.L. (1997). *Working with Natural Groups of Youth-at-risk*. Hong Kong: Chinese University of Hong Kong.

McDonald, R., Banks, S. and Hollands, R. (1993). "Youth and policy in the 1990s" *Youth and Policy*. Vol. 40: 1–9.

McWhirter, J., McWhirter, B., McWhirter, A. and McWhirter, E. (1998). *At-risk Youth: A Comprehensive Response*. (2/e) Pacific Grove, CA: Brooks/Cole Publishing Company.

Mok, H.F. (1999). "Youth policy in Hong Kong: an interpretation of hegemony" In J. Lee, S. Chiu, L.C. Leung & K.W. Chan (eds.) *New Social Policy*. Hong Kong: Chinese University Press, pp 357–374. (In Chinese).

Ng, A. and Man, P. (1985). *The Report on the Evaluation of Outreaching Social Work*. Hong Kong: Chinese University of Hong Kong.

Ng, A., Lau, T.S., Lu, A., Tsoi, R. and Wong K.H. (1975). *Social Causes of Violent Crimes among Young Offenders in Hong Kong*. Hong Kong: Chinese University of Hong Kong.

Paulu, N. (1987). *Dealing with Dropouts: The Urban Superintendents' Call to Action*. US: Department of Education.

Schervish, P. (1983). *The Structural Determinants of Unemployment: Vulnerability and Power in Market Relations*. New York: Academic Press.

Shi, L. (2001). "The convergence of vulnerable characteristics and health insurance in the US" *Social Science and Medicine*. Vol. 53(4): 519–29.

Social Welfare Department (2002). *Services for Young People*. <http://www.info.gov.hk/swd/html_eng/ser_sec/ser_young/index.html>

Taite, G. (1995). "Shaping the at-risk youth: youth, governmentality and the Finn Report" *Discourse: Studies in the Cultural Politics of Education*. Vol. 16(1): 123–34.

—— (2000). *Youth, Sex and Government*. New York: Peter Lang Publishers.

Townsend, P. (1981). *Poverty in the United Kingdom: A Survey of Household Resources and Standard of Living*. Berkeley: University of California Press.

Turner, B. (2001). "The end(s) of humanity: vulnerability and the metaphor of membership" *Hedgehog Review*. Vol. 3(2): 7–32.

Wikstrom, S. and Wikstrom, P. (2001). "Why are single parents more often threatened with violence? A question of ecological vulnerability" *International Review of Victimology*. Vol. 8(2): 183–98.

Wong, D. (1997). *Longitudinal Case Study on the Deviation Process of Youth-at-risk*. Hong Kong: Northern District Outreaching Social Work Team, Lutheran Social Services. (In Chinese)

Working Party on Review of Children and Youth Centre Services (1994). *Report on Review of Children and Youth Centre Services*. Hong Kong: Government Printer.

CHAPTER **10**

Burgess, E.W. (ed.) (1926). *The Urban Community*. Chicago: University of Chicago Press.

Capuzzi, D. and Gross, D.R. (eds.) (1996). *Youth at Risk: A Preventive Resource for Counselors, Teachers, and Parents*. (2/e) Alexandria, VA: American Counseling Association.

Chan, P.C., Kwok, N.Y., Choi, K.F. and Tsang, W.K. (eds.) (1997). *Outreaching Social Work in Hong Kong*. H. K.: Chap Yin.

Cloward, R A. and Ohlin, L.E. (1960). *Delinquency and Opportunity: A Theory of Delinquent Gangs*. New York: Free Press.

Cohen, R.K. (1955). *Delinquent Boys: The Culture of the Gang*. New York: Free Press.

Curtis, S. (1989). *Juvenile Offending: Prevention through Intermediate Treatment*. London: B. T. Batsford Ltd.

Dryfoos, J.G. (1990). *Adolescents At Risk: Prevalence and Prevention*. Oxford: Oxford University Press.

Durkheim, E. (1933). *The Division of Labor in Society*. (translated by Simpson, G.) New York: Free Press.

Gerard, R. (1970). Institutional Innovations in Juvenile Corrections. *Federal Probation*. Vol. 34(4): 37–44.

Glueck, S. and Glueck, E. (1956). *Physique and Delinquency*. New York: Harper.

Goddard, H. H. (1914). *Feeblemindedness: Its Causes and Consequences*. New York: Macmillan.

Hewitt, L. E. and Jenkins, R. L. (1946). *Fundamental Patterns of Maladjustment: The Dynamics of Their Origin*. Illinois: State of Illinois.

Inhelder, B. and Piaget, J. (1958). *The Growth of Logical Thinking from Childhood to Adolescence*. New York: Basic Books.

Jessor, R., Donovan, J.E. and Costa, F.M. (1991). *Beyond Adolescence: Problem Behavior, and Young Adult Development*. New York: Cambridge University Press.

Klein, M.W. (1971). *Street Gangs and Street Workers*. N. J.: Prentice-Hall, Inc.

Kohlberg, L. (1963). Moral Development and Identification. *Child Psychology: A Yearbook of the National Society for the Study of Education*. Chicago: University of Chicago Press: 277–333.

Kornhauser, R.R. (1978). *Social Sources of Delinquency: An Appraisal of Analytical Models*. Chicago: University of Chicago Press.

Lam, D. (1997). Relating with Marginal Youth in Hong Kong: A Process Reflection. *Youth and Policy Issues*. No.58: 39–56.

Lee, F.W.L. (1990). Intermediate Treatment and Outreaching Social Work. In Editorial Committee of Outreaching Journal (ed.) *The Practice of Outreaching Social Work in Hong Kong*. H. K.: Chap Yin P.276–84.

—— (1994a). Group Work with "Youth-at-risk". *Asia Pacific Journal of Social Work*. Vol. 4(2): 31–40.

—— (1994b). Police and Social Workers: The Possibility of Cooperation in Helping Juvenile Delinquents *Hong Kong Journal of Social Work*. Vol. 28(1): 77–83.

— (1996). Services for Young Offenders: The Way Ahead. *Youth Work in the 21ˢᵗ Century — Challenge, Change and Development.* (Resource Book on Children and Youth Services Vol. III) Children and Youth Division, HKCSS (ed.) H. K.: Chap Yin P.147–58.

— (2000). Working with Natural Groups of Youth-at-risk: An RGC Approach. *Groupwork.* Vol. 12(3): 21–36.

— (2002a). Push-Pull Theory of Youth Problems. In Lee, F.W.L. (ed.) *Hong Kong Youth Problems in the Early 21ˢᵗ Century — The Phenomena, Analyses and Solutions.* (in Chinese) Hong Kong: Hong Kong University Press. P.69–81.

— (2002b). Encounters Between Police and "Unattached Youth" and the "Occurrence of Juvenile Delinquency" *Police Practice and Research: An International Journal.* Vol. 3(2): 89–103.

Lee, F.W.L. and Cham, L.M.Y. (2002).The Possibility of Promoting User Participation in Working with High Risk Youth. *British Journal of Social Work.* Vol. 32: 71–92.

Lee, F.W.L., Lo, T.W. and Wong, D.S.W. (1996). Intervention in the Decision- making of Youth Gangs. *Groupwork.* Vol. 9(3): 292–302.

Lo, T.W. (1986). *Outreaching Social Work in Focus.* H. K.: Caritas-Hong Kong.

— (1992). Groupwork with Youth Gangs in Hong Kong. *Groupwork.* Vol. 5(1): 58–71.

— (1993). Neutralisation of Group Control in Youth Gangs. *Groupwork.* Vol. 6(1): 51–63.

McWhirter, J.J., McWhirter, B.T., McWhirter, A.M. and McWhirter, E. H. (1998). *At-Risk Youth: A Comprehensive Response.* (2/e) N. Y.: Brooks/Cole Publishing Company.

Merton, R. K. (1968). *Social Theory and Social Structure.* New York: Free Press.

Morris, T. (1957). *The Criminal Area: A Study in Social Ecology.* U. K.: Routledge And Kegan Paul.

National Institute of Mental Health (1970). *Report on the XYY Chromosomal Abnormality.* Washington, DC: U. S. Government Printing.

Park, R.E., Burgess, E.W. and McKenzie, R.D. (1925). *The City.* Chicago: University Of Chicago Press.

Philpott, W.H. (1978). Ecological Aspects of Anti-social Behavior. In Hippchen, L.J. (ed.) *Ecologic-Biochemical Approaches to Treatment of Delinquents and Criminals.* New York: Van Nostrand Reinhold: 116–37.

Piaget, J. (1948). *The Moral Judgment of the Child*. New York: Free Press.

Ray, J. and Kerslake, A. (1979). *Intermediate Treatment and Social Work*. London: Heinemann.

Regoli, R.M. and Hewitt, J.D. (2000). *Delinquency in Society*. (4/e) New York: Mc-Graw-Hill.

Rose, S.D. (1998). *Group Therapy with Troubled Youth: A Cognitive-Behavioral Interactive Approach*. London; SAGE Publications.

Schoenfeld, C.G. (1975). A Psychoanalytic Theory of Juvenile Delinquency. In People, E.E. (ed.) *Readings in Correctional Casework and Counseling*. CA: Goodyear: 24–6.

Spergel, I.A. (1995). *The Youth Gang Problem: A Community Approach*. N. Y.: Oxford University Press.

Sutherland, E. H. (1939). *Principles of Criminology*. (3/e) Philadelphia: Lippincott.

Tang, C.S.C. and Davis, C. (1997). *Study on the Risk and Protective Factors of Juvenile Gangs and Runaway Youth in Hong Kong*. Hong Kong: Authors.

Index